The Tribe

Stephen Shaw

The Tribe

ISBN: 978-0-9928042-3-7

Stephen Shaw's Books

Visit the website: www.i-am-stephen-shaw.com

I Am contains spiritual and mystical teachings from enlightened masters that point the way to love, peace, bliss, freedom and spiritual awakening.

Heart Song takes you on a mystical adventure into creating your reality and manifesting your dreams, and reveals the secrets to attaining a fulfilled and joyful life.

They Walk Among Us is a love story spanning two realities. Explore the mystery of the angels. Discover the secrets of Love Whispering.

The Other Side explores the most fundamental question in each reality. What happens when the physical body dies? Where do you go? Expand your awareness. Journey deep into the Mystery.

Reflections offers mystical words for guidance, meditation and contemplation. Open the book anywhere and unwrap your daily inspiration.

5D is the Fifth Dimension. Discover ethereal doorways hidden in the fabric of space-time. Seek the advanced mystical teachings.

Star Child offers an exciting glimpse into the future on earth. The return of the gods and the advanced mystical teachings. And the ultimate battle of light versus darkness.

The Tribe expounds the joyful creation of new Earth. What happened after the legendary battle of Machu Picchu? What is Christ consciousness? What is Ecstatic Tantra?

The Fractal Key reveals the secrets of the shamans. This handbook for psychonauts discloses the techniques and practices used in psychedelic healing and transcendent journeys.

My name is Adam. I was an archaeologist conducting research at Crystal Mountain in the Sahara Desert. That was before I met Ra, the sun-god. Now it seems like a lifetime ago.

So much has happened. I have been dragged kicking and screaming into a glorious spiritual adventure. Exposed to mystical teachings across the planet. Deeply immersed in a new way of life. Learned the value of spiritual and emotional maturity.

Survived the legendary battle of Machu Picchu.

Sadly, I said goodbye to my best friend, a mysterious monk named Śakra. More than a monk ... he was known as the Star Child ... and, along with his true love the Guardian of the Earth, he was a Watcher on this bruised and struggling planet. The good news is that he joined his true love in another dimension.

And such is life. It keeps moving forward. One chapter flows into another. The hardest lesson I had to learn over the last few years is 'Surrender'. Yep, that venerable truth. Surrender, trust and flow are imperative, because, as Ra so eloquently put it: *'The greatest truth you will ever know is that Life is breathing. In this very moment, in the Now, there is a simultaneous In-Breath and Out-Breath.'*

I am hoping you have met Ra, otherwise you have some catching up to do.

John Lennon, a musician from the distant past, once said: 'Life is what happens to you while you're busy making other plans.' That makes me smile. Indeed. You have to learn to surrender and flow.

Here I am, touring through South America. On the hunt for a woman who has entered my consciousness and somehow grabbed my heart. She has probably never heard of me. Ironic really. After all, she led a revolution: the March of the Women and Children, one of the prime instigators for global change.

As for me, all I did was meditate at Machu Picchu ... and miraculously, at a crucial point, managed to vanquish the darkest spirit ever to shadow our beautiful planet. Yep, that was me. I destroyed Apophis. Śakra simultaneously gave his life to save mine, thereby fulfilling a quietly camouflaged destiny.

I was supposed to become the leader of a free world. Who knew?

Now, with the dust clouds still settling over Machu Picchu, I am making my way to Brazil. I know she is the 'one', fated to be my first and last romantic relationship. According to Iboga, the wonderful prophetic South African shaman: 'The woman waiting for you is strong-willed, courageous, vulnerable and full of love. She lives with a wide open heart accepting whatever life offers her. A wonderful partner to build a new world.'

I can't wait to meet her.

My mind casts back to the eminent members of the Council of Light. What a privilege to have interacted with them. Sikh Nanak; Imam Abu Talib; Zen Master Koichi; Aboriginal Elder Mandu; South African Shaman Iboga; Hopi Mystic Qaletaqa; Klamath Elder Láshaltko; and Q'ero Shaman Chuya, who disappeared abruptly after the final battle against the darkness. Had to smile at the concomitant reports about a huge condor soaring through the Peruvian skies.

Ah, the Council.

Twelve religious leaders, spiritual teachers and enlightened masters. Selected because of their unconditional unwavering commitment to light, love and truth.

I sigh deeply. It's been an intense seven years. Enormous change and upheaval for people and planet. Only 5.5 billion humans remain. On the plus side, it's July 2030 and the Golden Age is finally upon us. We have collectively broken free of the dark lattice.

What does that mean?

In a word: Freedom

We now have unadulterated power to choose. No more negative influences. No more external interference. At last, we are truly the captain of our ship, and the master of our fate. The future is completely and utterly up to us.

Fortunately we are not alone. The gods of light, under the guidance of Ra, have committed to help rebuild our world, while ensuring that power and governance remain firmly in the hands of humans. It is the beginning of a new era of truth, freedom, peace, love and light.

So, what now? Where to from here?

First I have to find a woman. Eva Luria. The revolutionary leader I saw in the newsfeed. Long auburn hair, radiant blue eyes, beautiful smile. Heart of a warrior. Soul of an angel.

* * *

The newsfeed report originated from Brasilia, capital of Brazil, in the State of São Paulo. Once the plane touches down I quickly disembark. The last few years have taught me to travel light; only a trusty small suitcase accompanies me. No waiting for luggage to be offloaded onto the baggage carousel.

I make my way to the local news office and catch the tail of a frenetic editor. Yes, he remembers her. Vaguely recalls a snippet of information. "Get down to Rio. She was photographed taking a well-deserved break on Ipanema beach." Big smile. Gratitude. Brusque wave.

The short-hop flight from Congonhas Airport in São Paulo to Santos Dumont Airport in Rio de Janeiro takes 45 minutes. A taxi hugs the coastline for a further 20 minutes then drops me at my hotel in Leblon. The concierge issues some friendly advice: (a) Social inequality and poverty have the unfortunate consequence of a high crime rate, so take care; (b) Today, being a Sunday, the roadway alongside the beach is closed to motor vehicles, and people use the opportunity to roller skate, skateboard, ride bikes and enjoy leisurely strolls.

I nod respectfully, download the proffered e-pamphlet, and head for Avenue Delfim Moreira next to Leblon beach. Casting my sandals aside, I sink my toes into the soft sand. Ah, that luscious tickly feeling … warm sun soaking into my skin … deep breaths of fresh ocean air … seagulls cavorting in the brilliant sky.

Time to get the lay of the land. Open the e-pamphlet.

'Rio de Janeiro is the second largest city in Brazil. It has a tropical and temperate climate which means the city enjoys sunny skies and warm weather all year round. The temperatures stay around 25 degrees Celsius as an average low and 30 degrees Celsius as an average high … Winter is from June until August … slightly cooler than the height of summer, less humidity, less chance of rain.'

I scan the shimmering sands. Chances of me finding this woman.

Subtle sensation … familiar energy … a hint from beyond?

Oh yeah … what did Śakra teach me?

'You have to learn to trust your intuition. When you meet someone for the first time, you immediately encounter their energy field. Everything you need to know about that person is written in their energy. Your misinterpretations are usually the result of the mind's interference – assumptions and projections. You often get hurt when you ignore the intuitive voice – the voice of your soul. Equally, you are living and breathing in a Field of Energy which contains plenty of helpful information, including the whispers from the multi-dimensions. Learn to tap and absorb these messages.'

I need to track her energy. We have met before … once she entered my dreams … another time I fell into her bedroom while surfing the multi-dimensions … during a shamanic vision I noticed her calling me in the distance … then I saw her leading the March of the Women and Children via the newsfeed from South America.

Tapping my head. The key principle.

Aha.

'You are consciousness and your intention directs your journey.'

I shift my awareness and start walking.

Hmm … nothing here.

Leblon beach runs smoothly into Ipanema beach. My attention is drawn to a scantily clad group of roller skaters breezing along Avenue Vieira Souto … perusing the glistening bodies reposing

on the white sands ... absorbing the bright colours and joyful
energy ...

Glance at the e-pamphlet.

'Ipanema beach is located just south of Copacabana beach. The
area is renowned for its world-class restaurants, shops and cafes.
During winter strong wind and wild waves create optimal
surfing conditions with regular churning barrels. The sunsets are
often spectacular, encouraging spontaneous applause from the
locals.'

Applauding a sunset ... love it ...

Nearing the end of the fluttering sand, suddenly get a taste of her
energy ... drifts east then north ... aha ... increasing my stride ...
crossing over to Copacabana beach.

'Copacabana beach, 4 kilometres of pristine beauty located on the
Atlantic shore ... numerous hotels, restaurants, bars, night clubs
and residential buildings scattered along its promenade. Rio de
Janeiro celebrates New Year's Eve with a colossal fireworks
display at Copacabana Beach, and approximately two million
people crowd onto the warm moonlit sand to watch the
magnificent spectacle. Many famous musicians have held
concerts on this popular beach.'

Yes ... she was here ... playful, relaxed ... the energy moves onto
Avenue Atlantica alongside the beach ... speeds away ... did she
get into a taxi? ... where could she have gone?

Tummy rumbling. Sit down at a beach kiosk, order seafood salad,
consult the map.

It's a 15-minute drive to Sugarloaf Mountain ... I wonder ...

'Sugarloaf Mountain is a peak situated in Rio de Janeiro at the mouth of Guanabara Bay. To reach the summit, passengers use two cable cars: The first ascends to the shorter Morro da Urca, 220 metres high; the second ascends to Pão de Açúcar, 396 metres high. The glass-walled cable car or *teleférico* is capable of holding 65 passengers. The summit offers a panoramic view of the city and harbour, sweeping beaches, shimmering ocean and lush green hills.'

My food arrives. It's already late afternoon. I enquire about the famous sunset. Big smile. "6.30pm. Make the trip up to Pão de Açúcar in the next hour and you can watch the sun dance across the sky. Bom apetite!"

Appreciative nod. Easy decision.

Enjoying the slow crisp beer. Delicious sunrays peeking through the iridescent umbrella … delicately caressing my forearms … silver-tipped waves curling in the distance … soft breeze wafting across my face … eyes closing for a moment … sinking into pleasurable repose …

Cascading into my consciousness … her beautiful face … crystal clear … as if she is sitting right before me … I jolt to full wakefulness … she must be near!

Catching a taxi. Check the e-pamphlet. Gaze upward in anticipation. There's a cable car every twenty minutes. Sensing the thread of her energy. Climb aboard. The glass walls provide an amazing 360-degree view. Arriving at the summit. Oh, her energy is stronger. Wow. What a panorama. Breathtaking!

Sudden trepidation. I am a total stranger. Is she sensing my energy too? What if she has a romantic partner?

I walk toward the south end. A few tourists disperse. Could it be?

Leaning against the railing, bouncy auburn hair, curves in all the right places. She turns. Our eyes lock. My heart jumps. I know her. I *know* her.

Words disappear from my mouth.

She is first to speak. Hands on her hips. "Eu te conheço?" Portuguese. No idea. Slightly challenging stare. "Te conozco?" Spanish. Um, let me think. Still nothing. Finally, "Do I know you?"

Aha. Pull myself together. Trust the energy.

"Eva Luria?"

"Yes?"

"Adam Kadmon."

I extend my hand.

Shakes her head. Stares directly at me.

Then a ripple of luminous laughter. "I know who you are."

Relief flows over me. I manage a smile.

She steps forward and pulls me into a tight embrace. "I have waited a lifetime for you."

My heart is beating rapidly. Scent of her skin, softness of her hair, scintillation of her soul. Exhilarating floating feeling.

"Oh, the world is spinning!"

Good to hear. Not just me.

I take her hand and we watch the sky turn brilliant gold … then hues of red … eventually settling into deep mauve and purple.

"S-p-e-c-t-a-c-u-l-a-r!"

"Indeed."

Eva points directly west toward Corcovado Mountain. The white statue of Christ the Redeemer is lit up. Magnificent and inscrutable, the immense figure magnanimously overlooks the city.

"Wow!"

She smiles. "Although the statue is about 4 kilometres from here, it is easily seen. Located at the peak of the 700-metre mountain in the Tijuca Forest National Park, Christ the Redeemer is 30 metres tall, not including its 8-metre pedestal, and its arms stretch out 28 metres."

I can feel the energy shimmering between us. Something magical is happening. It's like meeting a best friend after a long time apart. Her essence is so similar to mine.

"Are we kindred spirits?" I venture.

"Is that more than a soul mate?"

"I think so."

She touches my cheek gently. "Then we are kindred spirits."

Her radiant blue eyes are warm and kind. I feel lost in them. If there is one truth I know, it's this: Eyes are the windows to the soul. Eyes keep no secrets. They reflect the essence of a being.

I gaze down her luscious body. Navy blue long-sleeve dress with flower imprints. The high heels make her the same height as me. Perfect.

I pull her in close and kiss her softly ... then a little passionately.

Clasp her hand. "So grateful we found each other."

The sky is painting a rainbow of luminous colours. For the longest time we stand enraptured, staring at Christ the Redeemer.

Finally she says: "Do you think anyone has worked it out yet?"

I cast my head back and smile. "No, but in time they will."

A serene stillness enfolds us.

Later we board the last cable car which leaves Pão de Açúcar at 8.40pm. Scattered below us are hundreds of twinkling lights, adorning the darkness like a bejewelled Brazilian necklace.

It's been a long day, so after a brief farewell and a promise to meet tomorrow, we are off to our respective hotels; mine in Leblon, hers in the adjoining borough of Ipanema.

Needless to say, I don't get much sleep.

* * *

In the morning I burst out of bed wide awake, fling the windows open, and breathe in the invigorating ocean air. My heart is beating wildly and happily. Samba is playing on the television and I have a little dance around the room.

The concomitant information reflects on the screen:

'Samba is a musical genre and dance style originating in Bahia, Brazil, but with strong African roots. It is recognised around the world as a symbol of Brazil and the Brazilian Carnival. Samba has become an icon of Brazilian national identity. *Samba carioca* is the samba that is played and danced in Rio de Janeiro.'

After a long hot shower, and light breakfast on the terrace, I activate the lume and give her a call. We agree to meet on Ipanema beach in a couple of hours.

The time drags. I find myself pacing. Are you supposed to be this excited when you meet someone you love? Oh my. Am I in love already? Is that possible?

Naturally I am the first to arrive, anxiously waiting on a promenade bench, my leg jittering like a nervous cat. How can I be feeling such mixed emotions?

There she is. I bound over, grab her in an affectionate embrace.

"I am so happy to see you."

A warm smile lights up her face.

"I am delighted to see you too."

She places her hand in mine and we stroll onto the scrunchy sand. A cool breeze wafts along the shore. A few surfers are carving turquoise waves. The shimmering sun is deliciously warming. Everything is so calm and peaceful.

We amble and talk for hours.

Eva is a woman driven by her spirit and heart. It's exceptionally beautiful. Kindness, caring and empathy are hallmarks of her inner essence. Passionate about people and planet, she campaigned tirelessly for social, political and economic justice, culminating in the now-famous worldwide March of the Women and Children. And it's not over. She is ready to build a new world.

I smile to myself. Eva Luria, my Brazilian goddess.

She asks about my life and experiences. I regale her with stories from my childhood in Italy. The importance of family and community. My brief career as an archaeologist before being whisked into a tempestuous spiritual adventure with Ra, Baset, Śakra and the Council of Light. Journeying across the world; sacred objects and psychedelic ceremonies; mysterious gods of light; legendary battle of Machu Picchu; destruction of the dark lattice.

"Impressive," she mutters softly.

"You have quite the history yourself."

She tilts her head. "And what have you learned?"

"The Star Child said '*The gods of light, the precursors of the great religions, the great spiritual teachers — they all taught the same things: loving-kindness, compassion, forgiveness, acceptance, equality, respect, responsibility, gratitude and service.*' Ra told me '*There is nothing more important than developing good character and spiritual maturity.*'

"Toward the end of my journey I finally understood the Sikh's mentorship toward exemplary character, the imam's teaching about good deeds, and the Ubuntu philosophy of the sangoma. It became obvious that spiritual maturity is the gateway to stepping into the worlds of energy and power. That is why initiations and impeccability tests exist."

Brief nod. "Interesting."

"Śakra also gave this valuable advice: *'Keep meditating as it naturally cultivates your sensitivity. Commit to living with impeccability. Align yourself with the beings of light that exist everywhere and everywhen. Great power results from initiating such an allegiance.'*

"Iboga taught the following: 'Ubuntu is a philosophy, an attitude, a way of life. Essentially it focuses on the power of relationships and allegiances. At an earthly level, this refers to keeping your connections clear of negative energy, living with forgiveness and loving-kindness, understanding that we are not alone in the Mystery, and working together for the benefit of humanity and our planet. The more powerful and wise sangomas also forge alliances with the beings of light in the multi-dimensions.'"

She smiles. "I like that."

"My final lesson was Love. Becoming immersed and engulfed in Love. Understanding Love in all its forms. Appreciating Love. Being Love. Acting with Love. Loving-kindness. Altruism."

Eva turns and gazes into my eyes. "You are a true kindred spirit."

We embrace tenderly. Hearts intertwining, souls joyously conversing. The longest precious moment ... Is this how romantic love feels? ... marvellous ... like coming home.

Later in the afternoon we catch a taxi to Avenue Infante Dom Henrique, about 15 minutes north along the coast. There is a restaurant called Porcão Rio's that Eva wants to show me. She explains: "Brazil is famous for the quality of its meat. This chain of Brazilian meat-grills or *churrascarias* works on an all-you-can-eat principle. The *rodizio* system means you pay a fixed price or *preço fixo* and the waiter brings samples of food at several times throughout the meal, until you signal that you have had enough. Porcão has branches in Barra da Tijuca and Ipanema, but the

Flamengo branch – known as Porcão Rio's – has floor to ceiling windows displaying a spectacular view of Sugarloaf mountain. The restaurant also has a buffet which offers salads, seafood, cheeses, olives and other treats."

In the early evening, replete and content, she shares a little surprise. "I have tickets to visit the Christ the Redeemer statue tonight. We just have to hop on a minibus."

Alright then. Up close and personal.

Soon we are making the short trip up Corcovado Mountain. It is already 6pm and the driver announces that the last bus leaves at 7pm. I am wondering if we have enough time to enjoy a viewing.

Cristo Redentor is awesome. As the sun disappears below the horizon, powerful spotlights dramatically illuminate the statue of Christ. Following his gaze across the city, a peculiar question ruffles my consciousness: Why the juxtaposition, why the disparity, of pleasure and poverty?

In the base of the statue is a small chapel with the capacity to accommodate 150 people. Without saying a word, Eva enters, makes the sign of the cross, then falls to her knees. Her prayers are silent, the energy intense. I feel strange and light-headed.

Half an hour later we are standing near the statue, admiring the magnificent view. The weather is balmy. It is a beautiful and serene night.

Her hand touches mine.

"Do you know today's date?"

"Um … 7 July?"

"7th of the 7th."

"Meaning?"

"Exactly one year ago the American Peace Organisation was formally ratified during the signing of the Peace Accord at the White House. The beginning of a true United America."

"I remember."

Why is she mentioning this? What is the significance of 7s?

Her energy field has shifted. Change of plans.

"You going to tell me what's happening?"

She smiles and touches my cheek.

"We are staying. Let the last bus depart."

"How? Surely they will inspect?"

Her left hand extends, revealing a ring of obsidian encompassed by fine silver.

Shrugging my shoulders in bewilderment.

She dials the silver circle and disappears.

Great. Thought those days were over.

Waiting patiently.

"Ta da!"

"Cute. You have a sacred object. Where did you get it?"

"A woman named Tefnut gave it to me."

"Athletic, slender build, redhead, intense green eyes?"

"Yes. You know her?"

That old feeling of higher orchestration is returning.

"When did she give it to you?"

"A few years ago. Said it would help me on my mission."

"And did it?"

"Saved my life a couple of times."

Wow. That cunning cat. It's all starting to make sense now. Ra explained to me that he had jumped into the Time Stream from the Time Chamber in the Temple of Arcturus, just as Apophis had done when he made his escape. He never mentioned that Baset was with him in the Time Chamber. She must have stealthily acquired Maya's time-dilation ring, then followed Ra into the Time Stream. Have to admire her brilliance.

I place my hand on Eva's shoulder.

"Tefnut is a goddess of light who prefers to take the form of a cat."

Her hand covers her mouth.

"Really? A cat?"

"A sleek bronze short-haired Egyptian Mau named Baset."

"The cat in your spiritual adventure?"

"Yes. Baset is the protector and defender of Ra. Also known as the Lady of Flame and Eye of Ra. Accompanies him everywhere."

"Hmm. Intriguing."

I fold my arms. "What's your plan?"

"We vanish while they are closing. Move forward a few hours. You'll need to hold my hand so we are both ensconced in the time-dilation field."

"Aha."

I smile. Time to surrender and flow.

Three hours later we are completely alone. I consult the lume: 10.25

"Do you mind if I meditate for a while?"

"Go ahead."

Sitting cross-legged, I silently chant the sacred mantra given to me by Śakra. There's a mysterious language that he knows, and certain words engender an exquisite thought-force. It's a whole other level of being.

Eventually I rouse and return to earthly reality.

She is staring at me. It's unsettling.

"What's up?"

"Just admiring my kindred spirit."

"What time is it?"

"10.55"

"How much longer?"

"I don't know."

"Okay."

I stretch my legs. Oh, that feels good.

She gestures with her eyes. "Let's walk to that vantage point, so we can look directly and comfortably at the face of Christ."

I nod and follow her.

We unfurl a blanket and lay down on our backs, gazing up at the magnificent statue.

The energy starts to feel rather surreal. A peculiar tension is percolating in the air. Becoming slightly light-headed again. I wonder what is happening.

Glance at the lume, check the time: 11.11

Suddenly an enormous bolt of lightning strikes each hand of *Cristo Redentor*, followed by a hair-raising *craaack!* I recoil at the thunderous noise. Immediately another colossal bolt ignites the head of Christ. Eva flinches and grabs my hand.

Then it all goes completely dark.

High above us ... strange twinkling ... faint movement in the heavens ... nebulous ... shooting stars ... descending illumination ...

She squeezes my hand. "Are those stars falling toward Earth?"

Bewildered. "I don't know."

Wait. They *are* falling toward us. Many are hurtling across the sky and some are getting perilously close. Should we move? Try to hide?

A single dazzling orb appears above the head of Christ.

I am filled with dread. Anxiety overtakes me. Reach to grab Eva's arm. "Dial the ring! Dial the ring!" She seems entranced. Wide-eyed. Unmoving. I am abruptly immobilised. Ugh ... watching helplessly as the brilliant orb hovers over Eva ... then me ... back to Eva ... swiftly plummets into her chest ... consternation ... struggling to break free ... sense the tears burning down my cheeks ...

When I awaken it is midnight. Without a thought, I rip the silver circle from my necklace and throw it to the ground. A loophole opens. Eva slumped in my arms, we jump through and land in my hotel room. Fortunately it is furnished with a king-size bed. I lay her down, remove her shoes, check her breathing, survey for wounds and marks – there are none; then cover her gently with the thin duvet.

Difficult choice. Call a doctor or wait and see? Was that something earthly or supernatural? The dark lattice is broken. Fear is a natural instinctive response. What does her energy field say? Ah, everything will be alright.

Sigh of relief.

Pulling a chair close to the bed.

Watching her intently.

Caressing her face.

An hour drifts by.

Eyes heavy …

Head bobbing …

Slide in next to her …

Surrendering to sleep.

* * *

The next morning I have many questions.

"How do you feel?"

"Fine."

"Are you in full health?"

"Yes."

Deep breath.

"Any wounds?"

"No."

"Compos mentis?"

"Huh?"

"You have control of your mind?"

She giggles.

"All is well. Perfect health."

"I was so worried. Only just found you. Don't want to lose you."

"Are you going to feed me? I'm very hungry."

"Yes, of course. We'll get room service. What shall I order?"

"You don't know?"

"Uh, no."

"Brazilian breakfast is called *café de monhã* or 'morning coffee'. Most people enjoy *pingado* which is sweetened coffee with warm milk served in a glass, preferably accompanied by *pão na chapa* or 'toasted bread rolls'."

"Alright."

"We also have a wide variety of locally available tropical fruit, like papaya and guaraná. And a very nutritious purple berry called açaí. Those ingredients make a delicious morning smoothie."

I order everything.

Half an hour later, breakfast trays on laps, still cosy under the duvet, we are happily chatting away.

"What on earth happened last night?"

She shrugs and flicks her hair. Her energy is slightly closed, wavering.

Hmm … I have learned not to push these situations. People share when they are ready. She is probably processing the highly unusual experience.

Deft change of topic.

"You know what's great?"

Shakes her head.

"Not only are we kindred spirits but aspects of our cultures are very similar."

"Really?"

"According to my lume, Brazilians focus much importance on the family structure. Families are often large, and even extended family members are close with one another. Italians are the same. Family is our heart-centre; we help and support each other, eat meals together and generally stay emotionally connected. Brazilians are affectionate, tactile, expressive people. Just like Italians. We are both straight-talkers, avoiding subtext and ambiguity. And over 80% of our respective populations are Catholic."

She nods. "Interesting."

"And then there's coffee! You have the *pingado*; we invented the *cappuccino*. Would you like to hear the backstory?"

"Sure."

"Cappuccino is an Italian coffee drink which is prepared with espresso, hot milk and steamed-milk foam. The name comes from the Capuchin friars, founded in 1520, who chose a particular design for their order's robes both in colour and shape of the hood. The Capuchins were an offshoot of the Franciscans, founded in 1208 by St Francis of Assisi.

"Originally the four great mendicant orders were the Carmelites (White Friars, founded in 1155, white cloak covering brown habit), the Franciscans (Grey Friars, founded in 1208, undyed habit), the Dominicans (Black Friars, founded in 1216, black mantle worn over white habit), and the Augustinians (Black friars, founded in 1244, black habit).

"In order to distinguish themselves, the new order chose a brown robe with a pointed hood, the latter being the mark of a hermit, signifying a commitment to poverty. The Italian word for hood is *cappuccio* and these friars became known as the Capuchins.

"The word *cappuccino* is a diminutive form of *cappuccio*. Our delicious coffee drink reminds us of the 'little hood' of the Capuchins and the brown colour of their robes, and encourages us to reflect on spiritual values in the midst of modern life."

Kind smile. "A daily contemplation."

"Exactly."

"What does 'mendicant' mean?"

"Mendicant orders are religious orders depending entirely on charity. They do not own property, either individually or collectively. A friar is a member of a mendicant order. Friars are different to monks as the former vow to serve society and the latter tend to commit to a cloistral life. Monks and nuns are usually rooted in a particular community or place. Friars have an itinerant evangelical lifestyle and travel across a wide geographical area. They are devoted to poverty, prayer and preaching, thereby emulating the life of Jesus."

Quizzical expression crosses her face. Eyes slowly closing. Her voice softens.

"Jesus Christ was not an evangelist. He did not seek to convert anyone to a religion. Neither was he a preacher. He had no church, no habit, no rules, no rituals."

The atmosphere has become surreal.

"He was a free agent. A being of light who knew God and came to master Love. He was tested on Earth. Stretched, challenged, pushed to the limits. All his teachings and parables intended to help people find the Light within and walk in unconditional Love."

Wow.

"He gave up his life for Love. Made the ultimate sacrifice and entered the kingdom of Heaven."

"The kingdom of Heaven?"

"Unless a person dies and is born again, he or she will not enter the kingdom of Heaven."

I swallow cautiously.

"What do you mean?"

"There are only two paths to enlightenment: Love and Awareness. He chose Love and came Home."

"Okay ..."

"To truly Love you have to die to your self; to be fully Aware you will lose everything and find emptiness. Two paths, same destination. Either way, your consciousness enters the kingdom of Heaven. You come Home."

She giggles cheerfully.

"Have you forgotten the teachings?"

Frowning and rubbing my eyebrow.

"Love has different degrees and stages, each one drawing you deeper like a moth to a flame until you are completely burned and no longer exist. You become Love. You are Love.

"Awareness is like water: transparent, flowing, yielding, empty, hard to grasp. When you look for Awareness, there is nothing to see; when you listen for it, there is nothing to hear."

"Where does this information originate?" I enquire gently.

"You are Consciousness and you are listening to yourself."

I take a deep breath. Something profound must have happened last night. She is exuding highest knowledge and deepest wisdom.

Suddenly her eyes burst wide open.

"Hey ... I could really use another pingado."

Startled. Feel slightly stunned.

"Are you aware of teaching me about Jesus Christ?"

"Hmm? When?"

"A moment ago."

Her brow furrows.

"Come on. Let's have another coffee."

I call room service then touch her hand gently.

"You closed your eyes and gave an enthralling discourse about Jesus Christ."

"You're amusing. I just blinked."

"Honestly."

"Are you sure? I don't remember."

"This must be connected to last night. What do you recall?"

Ruffling her long hair.

"Um ... bright orb ... hovering ... unable to move ... rush of energy ... everything becomes pure light ... woke up here in bed."

"That's it?"

Gazes at the ceiling.

"Had a weird dream."

"Tell me."

"Night sky ... blanket of twinkling stars ... huge fireworks ... thunderous noise ... dazzling Jenday Conures chirping in the heavens ... vast flock ... 144,000 ..."

"Jenday Conures?"

Eyes closing again.

"The Jenday Conure or jandaya parakeet is a small neotropical parrot with green wings and tail, reddish-orange body, yellow head and neck, and black bill. It is endemic to wooded habitats in north-eastern Brazil. Also known as the Flaming Conure, this highly intelligent bird adores fresh fruits, seeds and nuts; yet is hypersensitive to chocolate, caffeine and avocados."

"Alright."

Eyes flick open.

Should I even ask?

She continues with the dream. "A single bird ... brilliant plumage ... wings blurring ... staring at me with its dark eyes ... decision ... ecstatic merging ..."

Knock on the door. Bound over. Another tray of coffee and smoothies.

Luscious blue eyes smile. "Perfect. Thank you."

I lean out the window and stare at the shimmering ocean ... relishing the melange of clement ripples and curling waves ... the sun dances a samba across my face ... fill my lungs and exhale the sweet air.

After a few minutes I settle on the bed and savour my warm cappuccino.

Hmm ... I wonder ...

"Eva, will you do me a favour? Close your eyes and tell me what you know about coffee."

"Why?"

"Humour me."

She closes her eyes. I activate the lume to record her voice.

"Coffee is a beverage brewed from the roasted or baked seeds of several species of an evergreen shrub. The red or purple fruit of the coffee plant is referred to as a coffee cherry or berry. The seed inside the fruit is called a coffee bean. Once ripe, coffee berries are picked, processed and dried to yield the beans inside. The beans are roasted to varying degrees, depending on the required flavour, then ground and brewed to create coffee.

"Coffee plants are cultivated in more than 50 countries, predominantly in equatorial Latin America, Southeast Asia and Africa. Green (unprocessed, unroasted) coffee is one of the most traded agricultural commodities in the world. The leading producer of green coffee is Brazil (34%), followed by Vietnam (12%), Colombia (9%), Indonesia (6%) and Ethiopia (5%).

"The two most economically important coffee plants are *Coffea arabica* or Arabica and *Coffea canephora* or Robusta. Arabica comprises about 75% of worldwide coffee production; its beans generate a flavourful aromatic coffee with 0.8-1.4% caffeine. Robusta comprises about 20% of worldwide coffee production; its beans generate a bitter coffee with 1.7-4.0% caffeine. Green Robusta beans are typically 40-50% cheaper than Arabica beans."

Studiously tapping my lips. Is this information coming from her?

Let me expand the question.

"Where did coffee originate?"

Thoughtful breath.

"Ethiopia is the genetic birthplace of *Coffea arabica*, where it has been growing wild for millennia. Coffee cultivation, roasting and brewing first took place in southern Arabia in the 15th century, in the Sufi Muslim monasteries around Mocha in Yemen. Sufism is the inner, mystical dimension of Islam; once again we find an interesting spiritual connection with coffee."

Have to smile. Contemplation over a Caffè Mocha or Mocha Latte?

"By the 16th century, coffee had spread across the Middle East, Persia, Turkey and northern Africa. Flourishing trade between the Middle East, northern Africa and Venice brought coffee to Italy and the rest of Europe. In 1600, coffee was endorsed as a Christian beverage by Pope Clement VIII. In 1727, coffee was introduced to Brazil with committed cultivation commencing in 1822. Sadly, vast swathes of rainforest were cleared for coffee plantations, initially near Rio de Janeiro and later São Paulo."

I whistle softly. Eva's eyes flutter open.

"You ready?"

"Huh?"

"To hear about coffee?"

"You already answered the question."

I play back the recording.

Mouth agape.

"When did I say all that?"

"A few moments ago."

"I don't remember."

Raising my palms.

Growing silence.

Finally, "What is going on? I close my eyes and reveal a truth?"

"Seems so. Want to try again?"

Frowns. "Okay."

Eyes closing.

"Tell me about the best coffee in the world."

Hesitant quietude.

"Flavour and aroma preferences are subjective. However, the general consensus among humans is that Ethiopia produces the most flavoursome coffees, followed by Kenya and Columbia, and then Guatemala.

"Guatemala generates sweet and balanced coffees. Colombia has an abundance of microclimates and offers a range of unique flavour profiles. Kenya produces exquisite coffees, often with a delectable red berry and blackcurrant sweetness. Ethiopian coffees exude sweet cherry notes and delicate floral aromas, and are generally experienced as the best coffees in the world."

She opens her eyes.

"Well?"

"Listen for yourself."

A few moments pass.

"Still can't believe it."

I shrug my shoulders.

"The mystical event at *Cristo Redentor*?"

She jumps out of bed and stretches.

"I need a shower and a walk on the beach."

I place the trays on the table and repose on the bed. Steam is billowing from the washroom. A lyrical fusion of samba and jazz is streaming from her lume.

It looks like the day is just getting started.

* * *

Nature is truly wonderful ... refreshing breeze teasing our skin ... sand scrunching beneath our toes ... waves gently caressing the shore ... recharging our minds ... revitalising our bodies.

Why is nature soothing? Is it the result of negative ions exuded by forests, waterfalls and oceans? Negative ions are odourless, tasteless, invisible molecules that we inhale in abundance in certain natural environments. Once these ions reach our bloodstream, they produce biochemical reactions that increase levels of the neurotransmitter serotonin, which alleviates depression and stress, and contributes to feelings of well-being and happiness.

Perhaps the answer is more spiritual. Nature is uncorrupted by socio-cultural norms and media influences. It is not trying to be anything. It does not wallow in the past nor cogitate about the future. It dwells in the Now, fully present with what Is.

When you meet a hundred-year-old tree, you cannot help but gaze at its magnificence. After everything it has witnessed it still holds a regal and tranquil pose. Steadfastly refusing the capricious energy of humans, it graciously emanates dignity and stillness.

Flowers gift their gorgeous colours and delightful scents. Fruits proffer their succulent flavours and delicious juices. Butterflies flutter by, imprinting a psychedelic world upon our senses.

"Freedom," I mutter softly.

"Hmm?"

"Just thinking about nature. The joy and peace it brings. And the freedom."

"I adore trees. Love to be surrounded by them."

Glance into her blue eyes.

"Where is home for you? São Paulo? Rio?"

"Home is where the heart resides."

"Sweet."

"I mean it. You are my kindred spirit. We belong together. Home is you … and nature."

"Fair enough. And where is that?"

"Where do you want it to be?"

I stare at the twinkling white sand.

"Perhaps we need to consult Ra."

"The sun-god?"

"Yes."

"What has he to do with this?"

Shifting uncomfortably.

"Eva, I have a mission. To rebuild the world."

She slows her walking and clasps my hands.

"Adam, we have the same mission. Choosing a home is our decision."

It's true. Maybe I have spent too many years with the gods. What did Ra share when we first met? Oh yeah. *'We eventually understood that godly leaders and priests create disempowered and dependent peoples who no longer embrace autonomy and responsibility nor progress spiritually.'*

Nothing should interfere with the principles of unconditional love and responsibility for self, others and the planet. Following those guidelines, Ra promised to help rebuild our world while ensuring that power and governance remain firmly in the hands of humans.

Time to grow up. I have been a lone ranger for too long. This is my first and last romantic relationship. We must take care of each other.

"You are my family, Eva. We'll work it out together."

Heartfelt countenance.

"That's what I wanted to hear."

Deep breath.

"I have travelled all over the planet in the last few years. Not so keen on the UEMEA. It has been ravaged and reconstructed by Apophis."

Quizzical expression.

"United Europe, Middle East and Africa."

"Oh."

"I am more drawn to United America. You are a citizen of the UA. If we get married, I can stay here permanently."

"If?"

I smile. "When."

She prods me in the ribs. "Is that a proposal?"

"Uh ... no ..."

"Good answer. Hoping for something more romantic."

"A home on either the north or south continent will be great."

Fingertip stroking her lip.

"Perhaps a fresh location for both of us ... North America."

"Yeah, why not?"

"We should visit Ra anyway. If he is part of the dream, we'll need to have a conversation."

"You want to chat with Tefnut, no doubt."

Slow nod. "That too."

"Alright, that's settled. A conversation with the gods. A romantic proposal. Settle down in North America."

She hurls her arms around me, radiant eyes gazing intently.

"When do we commence?"

"How about tomorrow?"

"Purrfect."

"Did you say 'purrfect'?"

"Of course."

Her lips touch mine.

The cosmic dance begins.

* * *

We decide to spend the night at the hotel in Ipanema. There is no point staying in separate venues. I had already checked out of my hotel in the morning and stored my suitcase at reception. Travelling light has its advantages.

The evening is beautiful. A first quarter moon is hanging in the dusky sky, illuminating the beach and painting the churning waves silver. The waiter is setting down the tray of champagne and strawberries outside on the balcony. Sure, it's a bit decadent but I believe we have something to celebrate.

Reposing comfortably on cushioned loungers, we clink our flutes melodiously. "To kindred spirits and deepest love."

"That's beautiful, Adam."

I take a long sip.

"Do you know this is my first relationship? I had no romantic inclination until you entered my consciousness."

"Oh. When was that?"

"A few years ago. In a dream."

"How interesting."

"When it happened, Śakra told me that our paths were intersecting. That I was starting to sense your energy."

"I was beginning to sense yours too."

"How weird. Don't really understand it."

"Did Śakra give you any advice?"

Casting my mind back.

"Um … he said … '*Best thing to do is fully accept yourself, radiate your inner light and trust that the right partner will gravitate toward you.*'"

"Wise being."

"Indeed."

"Do you miss him?"

"Every day."

I stifle a tear.

She places her hand gently on mine.

"All will be well."

We survey the darkening ocean.

Eventually a contented sigh.

"Saved the best for last."

I glance at her curiously.

"Kindred spirits!"

"Ah."

She raises her glass again.

"To the magic and mystery of our love."

Ebullient clink.

A thought sparks in my mind. I wonder …

"Perhaps we can discover some truth about our situation."

"Yeah? How?"

Nonchalant shrug.

"Try closing your eyes again."

Ponders for a moment.

"Alright. Provided you record everything on the lume."

Rubbing my hands together.

"Ooh, I'm a little excited now."

"Hey, don't pressure me. No expectations."

"Absolutely."

Flute down. Eyes closing.

Hmm … How shall I proceed?

"Is Eva the 'one' for me?"

"Yes."

"What does the 'one' mean?"

Serene giggle.

"What does it mean to you?"

"Um … the ideal or optimal partner."

"There you go."

"How does this meeting occur?"

"Your life is a journey of consciousness. As your resonance shifts, you attract concomitant beings into your reality."

"You mean like a magnet? Or a tuning fork?"

"It is not even a journey. You are consciousness and you merely shift your perspective. When your perspective shifts, you meet consciousness of similar resonance."

Wow.

"Each reality is boundaried by a collective consciousness. As your perspective shifts, you move closer to your reality's boundary. You approach a transition. The closer you move to the edge, the less beings you encounter."

Struggling to keep up.

"How does this relate to souls?"

"A soul is a point of boundaried consciousness."

Studiously tapping my head.

"I don't understand."

Placid sigh.

"Do you recall the fundamental teaching of Ra?"

"I do. *'The greatest truth you will ever know is that Life is breathing. In this very moment, in the Now, there is a simultaneous In-Breath and Out-Breath.'*"

"Exactly. So, what is the Out-Breath?"

"The Source manifesting countless dimensions and infinite realities. The act of Creation."

"Try to imagine this unmanifested underlying Is-ness exploding a zillion pieces of light out of its cosmic mouth. Every piece of light is a point of consciousness. Humans call these 'souls'; in truth, they are merely single points of consciousness."

"Got it."

"Every point of consciousness is a minute fragment of the Source. Every point of consciousness is a creator. Actually, the Creator. These raw inexperienced souls begin to manifest thoughts and ideas. Creating the Dream you call Life."

Ruffling my hair.

"Isn't it lonely being a solitary point of consciousness?"

Eva claps her hands jubilantly.

"Yes, of course!"

"Aha."

"Every point of consciousness is on a journey back to the Source; in fact, a return to Itself, to unmanifested Is-ness. This naturally correlates with death of the illusory self and dissolution of all its dreams. Until this return occurs, each point of consciousness experiences separation and existential loneliness. In a sense, the deepest pain."

Understanding sparks in my mind.

"And we search for companions to fill the void."

She nods ardently.

"Depending on the energy you are carrying, or more precisely, the perspective of your consciousness, you will attract beings of similar resonance. Hence, you have soul mates that accompany you on your journey."

"Soul mates?"

Forbearing sigh.

"Let's go back a few steps. Every point of consciousness is in a constant cycle of manifesting-experiencing-manifesting-experiencing. This is living. This is creating. This is Life. Part of this dreaming involves manifesting-experiencing to fill the existential void. So you gravitate toward other points of consciousness that can (a) assuage the heartache (b) assist you with particular dream-cycles."

"Hence, the resonance."

"Yes, Adam."

Captivated attention.

"If your dream-cycle moves in a new direction, the aligned points of consciousness have to choose whether to change direction with you or risk the pain of separation. This fundamental decision underlies all Life."

"Ouch."

"Soul mates are points of consciousness that have chosen to remain aligned to similar dream-cycles and avoid the pain of separation. They travel through realities together. If one soul shifts to a higher perspective, it reaches down and assists the others. Soul mates form particularly strong bonds."

2 222

"Are souls male and female?"

"Of course not. A soul is just a point of consciousness. Human bodies have male-female aspects. Incarnating into a particular body creates a particular dream-cycle. One soul can incarnate into various human bodies over many lifetimes, continually changing gender, race, ethnicity, geographical location, and so on."

"Why do souls incarnate on Earth?"

"Why do souls incarnate in any reality?"

"To create and expand dream-cycles."

"Indeed."

"How many lifetimes do we have?"

"One life, many dreams."

"What about birth and death?"

Shakes her head calmly.

"There is no birth or death. You are an eternal being. You are merely closing and opening the doors of your perception."

Wow. Cappuccino contemplation.

Questions flicker across my mind.

"What is a kindred spirit?"

"Two souls who make the ultimate pledge: To walk the path of Love together. This is more than the friendship of soul mates. It is the bonding of two souls *as well as* the shared intention to focus on the dream-cycle of Love."

"So they are committing to each other *and* to manifesting-experiencing Love."

"Exactly."

"I have heard the term 'twin souls'. What is that?"

"A mythological romantic story created by humans. The mistaken idea that every soul is cleaved into a male and female aspect, then forced to evolve separately over many lifetimes, before being reunited in a final lifetime, and afterward ascending together to God."

"Sounds cruel and painful."

"The flaws are obvious. Souls have no gender. Souls are already single units. How can you split a point of consciousness? The myth ignores a fundamental truth: Every point of consciousness has free will. The power to create its own destiny. To be with whomever it chooses."

"That makes more sense."

"Kindred spirits have committed not only to each other but also to exploring, living, experiencing and manifesting Love. That is the secret ingredient of their heartfelt and passionate relationship."

"You are consciousness and your intention directs your journey."

"Precisely."

"Are kindred spirits from the same soul group?"

"Mostly. Soul mates are already sharing similar dream-cycles. So kindred spirits often arise from the same soul group. You could

---

say that two soul mates are taking their relationship to the next level."

"I like that."

"However, two souls from disparate soul groups, yet who have similar resonance, may choose to become kindred spirits. The key factors are their commitment to each other *and* to Love."

"Eva and I have a mission on Earth."

"Be careful, Adam. As kindred spirits your first priority is the dream-cycle of Love. Your mission is always secondary."

"Oh."

"In fact, the first priority for every point of consciousness is personal evolution, shifting of perspective, journeying toward the Source. Then manifesting-experiencing dream-cycles. And finally a mission, if there is one."

"Aha."

"Beings who confuse the sequence tend to lose their way."

Huge yawn. Suddenly realise how tired I am.

"Deeply grateful for the teachings."

Her eyes flutter open.

"Did it work?"

I burst into laughter.

"You have no idea."

We spend the next hour listening to the illuminating words, munching on strawberries and dark chocolate, and enthusiastically discussing the concepts.

Eventually we fall onto the soft bed. I cuddle her closely while she drifts off.

Unruffled whisper: "I love you, my kindred spirit."

My heart dances happily. I am asleep.

* * *

Sunrays are cascading across the ochre duvet. Brilliant blue sky is shimmering. I gaze at her sleepy face then kiss her gently on the lips.

Sapphire eyes squinting.

"Hey ..."

"Morning, beautiful person."

"Do I know you?"

"I hope so."

"Lover? Soul mate? Kindred spirit?"

"Uh ... all of the above."

"My soul mate would be offering me a steaming pingado."

I reach over and place a tray on the bed.

"Brazilian breakfast or *café de monhã*. Guess that makes me your kindred spirit."

Convivial smile.

"It does indeed."

She nips to the washroom. I arrange the pillows for sitting.

Within minutes she is ensconced and cosy.

"Thank you, meu amor."

I wait while the caffeine and sugar kicks in.

"Boom! There it is."

"What?"

I throw my head back and laugh.

"Ha-ha-ha-ha! Ha-ha-ha-ha!"

She looks at me strangely.

"What's with you?"

Playful shrug.

"Just happy I guess."

Naughty glint in her eyes.

"You said 'all of the above'?"

"Uh huh."

"Do you love me?"

"With all my heart."

"And all your soul?"

"With my entire being. You are my 'one'."

She pulls her nightshirt up over her head and casts it aside.

Staring at her luscious naked body.

"This is yours. Always will be."

"Beautiful and alluring."

She smiles brazenly.

"Brazilians are passionate and adventurous lovers. We are comfortable being naked. In the bedroom we enjoy uninhibited freedom."

"Seductively liberating."

"Am I your first?"

"My first and last; my one and only."

Contented sigh.

"When we make love, relish every moment, savour every sensation. The two most important guidelines are (a) presence (b) proceed slowly."

"Presence?"

She nods amiably.

"Whether it is kissing, fondling, stroking, licking ... we need to be fully present and undistracted. We make love with our entire beings or not at all. It is imperative that we invite mind, heart and spirit to the sacred event."

"And slowly?"

"Slowness increases awareness ... keeps us present ... allows us to assimilate every sensation. This is not a race; there is no finish line. It is not about orgasm; it is about pleasure."

"The keystone of Love, lover and pleasure."

"Exactly the right focus."

"Anything else?"

"The third important guideline is (c) freedom."

"Freedom?"

"Just remember two simple rules: Do what you want. Ask for what you want."

"How does that relate to freedom?"

"Sex is a flow of loving pleasurable energies. It is about vulnerability and surrender. The opening of the lotus flower. If we are constantly asking for permission or forgiveness, the flow is impeded. It is the responsibility of both lovers to follow their desires and express their needs clearly."

"What if you do something I don't like?"

"Every person has different physical, psychological and emotional pleasure zones. In time, these will be known by the lovers. However, pleasure zones can evolve over the years. Also, sensitivity can shift from day to day and moment to moment, so it is essential to communicate with your lover."

"Ah. I can just say 'no'."

"Better to say 'no, thank you' or utter an agreed safe word."

"Sounds more polite and comfortable."

"If the lover speaks the word, it should not be taken personally. It is not a rejection. Simply respect the flow of the lover and flow of sensations."

"What's our safe word?"

"How about 'no' in Portuguese: 'não'?"

"Pronounced 'now'?"

"Yes. But we'll make it sound like 'miaow'."

"An unhappy cat?"

"Uh huh."

I tilt my head and laugh.

"That's so funny!"

We bounce "niaow" back and forth a few times.

Suddenly her hands are stroking my face. An impassioned sexy look in her eyes.

Draws my head down to her full breasts.

"Lick them gently all over. Then move to my nipples. Soft sucking and nibbling."

Instinctively I want to ask 'Are you sure?' but the guidelines are clear and my mouth is engaged. Perhaps that is why she commenced in this way.

Her skin is velvety and delectable. I hear hushed moaning. It makes me feel aroused.

Scattering slow wet kisses upon her tummy ...

Glancing at the painted toenails ...

Tracing a path from her feet ...

Fingers delicately massaging ...

Gentle kisses up to her knees ...

Taking my time ...

Enjoying the sensuous journey ...

Languid licking along her inner thighs ...

Pleasurable gasps ...

Pulls her knees up ... spreads her legs ...

Wow. That is beautiful.

As if reading my mind, "Pussy."

Subtle nod.

Stroking her delicate hairs ...

Teasing her tumescent lips with tender kisses ...

Caressing her satiny inner thighs ...

Glistening wetness ... fragrant scent ...

Her fingers clasping my head ...

"Flat tongue not pointed tongue. As if licking an ice cream."

Aha.

Mmm ... savouring the sexy taste and silky texture ...

Her soft groans arousing me ...

Coaxing my head upward ...

"Between my lips near the top ... that fleshy protrusion ... my most sensitive area ..."

Pausing ... locating ... ah ...

"Clitoris ... draw the hood back ... the tip ranges from excruciatingly sensitive to deliciously sublime ... lap around the shaft mostly ... it's a delicate and intuitive dance ..."

Gasping ... writhing ... moaning ... fingers ruffling my hair ...

Energy intensifying ... something magical in the air ...

"Oh … oh … oh, oh, oh, ohhhhhhhh!"

Wow!

Elated smile.

Pulling me close … tender embrace … loving kisses …

"That was wonderful, Adam."

Gazing into her satisfied eyes.

"Glad you enjoyed it."

After a few minutes she pushes me off and rolls onto her tummy.

"Ready for round two?"

Beaming a huge smile.

"Oh yeah."

Softly biting her neck and shoulders …

Plentiful pleasurable purring …

Her skin is much softer than mine. And resplendently hairless. Women are truly sumptuous creatures. I wonder if she finds my body attractive?

Presence … mind, heart and spirit focus …

Travelling down her graceful back …

Leaping again to her ankles …

Caressing her supple calves …

Lapping the back of her thighs …

Staring at her beautiful pear-shaped bottom …

She arises onto hands and knees …

Instantly transforms from gorgeous to sexy.

"Wow!"

The view is spectacular and incredibly arousing.

Glistening pussy, rounded cheeks, rosy anus.

Gently licking her bottom …

Nibbling and caressing …

Soft groans.

Oh, she likes it.

Moment of hesitation.

Rule: Do what you want.

Trust, surrender and flow.

Circling my tongue around her anus.

Dulcet moaning.

Take the plunge. Slow sensual ice cream licks.

"Oh. Oh. Oh yes!"

Fondling her cheeks …

She reaches under the pillow. Squeezes strawberry-scented lubricant onto her fingers.

Reaches past her tummy …

Touching herself …

"Oh, don't stop!"

Tongue lusciously nuzzling.

Her bottom is quivering.

Energy intensifying.

"Oh … oh … oh …"

Deliriously sexy and wild.

"Oh … oh … Ohhhh!"

Wow!

She collapses onto her tummy.

"Lay on top of me. Put yourself inside me."

"Uh … you mean …"

Giggles.

"Front door. Back door is closed."

I slide into her succulent pussy.

"Oh my ..."

"Does that feel good?"

"Exquisite!"

She gets back up on all fours.

"Now fuck me."

"What?"

"I've had two orgasms. Forget about me. Chase your own pleasure."

All this pent-up energy. Racing horse released from the starting-gate. Grabbing her hips, riding into the satiny sleek tunnel, tantalising, exhilarating, mind-bending, scrumptiously satisfying, engulfing my being in cascading delight.

Suddenly hear myself shouting.

"Oh my ... Eva! Eva! Eva!"

I burst into tears.

After a minute she disengages, lays on her back and pulls me close.

Holding me tenderly, kissing my forehead.

It is a long while before I am able to speak.

Eventually, "That was beautiful, Eva."

She squeezes me affectionately.

"Love, lover and pleasure."

Ah yes. Our dream-cycle.

I smile. My eyes close.

Drift blissfully away.

* * *

It is late in the afternoon when I awaken. Eva is sitting by the window perusing a hologram on her lume. She looks fresh and vivacious.

"Hey, gorgeous man."

"Hey … Did I really sleep that long?"

"Yep. Had to check your pulse a couple of times."

I cast her a mock smile.

"Better drag my dishevelled body into the shower."

She sniffs and wrinkles her nose.

"Ha-ha-ha. Very funny."

"You're a bit moody."

"Yeah. Hungry I guess."

"I'll bet you are."

She winks at me.

My cheeks flush.

Stride over to her, gently touch her shoulder.

"Just wanted to say …"

"Hmm?"

"Making love with you was truly wonderful."

"Love is the operative word."

"I understand that."

"Won't happen again if you don't shower."

Bound over to the washroom and turn the mixer tap.

Frothy shave, inspect the skin, pluck a rogue hair.

Ah, one of the truly great pleasures in life. They should invent a
Do Not Disturb sign for the shower door. Don't even talk to me
when I am in here. No singing, no chatting, no thinking. Just the
sound and sensation of water cascading lavishly over my body.
A steamy, billowing meditation.

Dry the hair, spray underarms, moisturise the face.

What to wear today …

"Sweetheart, come here."

She is sitting on the edge of the bed. Familiar look in her eyes.

Rips the towel from my hips. Standing naked before her.

"You're going to love this."

"What?"

She wraps her soft luscious mouth around me.

"Oh my!"

Eyes rolling in my head.

Grips my bottom with one hand.

"Oh ..."

Legs quivering. Exquisite sensations.

I hear myself shouting again.

It's over in three minutes.

"Wow, that was intense."

"In a good way?"

Satisfied smile.

"Oh yeah."

"Right, back to the washroom. Then let's get out of here."

"Good plan."

We spend the rest of the day ambling along the twinkling Ipanema and Copacabana beaches, savouring the scarlet sunset, and dining al fresco under the shimmering stars.

Staring into her enchanting blue eyes.

What a wonder to have found her. This mystery of life. Journey of consciousness. Intention. Perception. Resonance. And always the choices. Choices, choices, choices. The foundation of existence, of every journey, of every reality, of every creation.

A small tear escapes my eye.

She wipes it with her thumb.

"You okay, sweetheart?"

"Deliriously happy."

Interlude of quietude.

"Do you think we should go visit Ra?"

I nod reflectively.

"Yes, it's about time."

"Shall we pack tonight?"

"It will take me two minutes."

She activates the lume to book a flight.

My hand reaches out.

"No need for that."

"Hmm?"

Jingling my necklace.

"What is it?"

"These are all sacred objects."

"Really? Like my ring?"

"Yep."

"Why so many?"

"It's a long story. There's a lot to share."

I spread the nine ornaments on the table.

"That's the Adi Shakti ... the Vajra ... the Bell ... the Loophole ... the Phoenix ... the Koan ... the Dart ... the Tantra Stone ... and the Rainbow Feather. Ra owns the Staff of Light, the Mezuzah and the Ring of Ezekiel."

"Twelve sacred objects."

"All belonging here on Earth."

"And my ring?"

"It originates from Arcturus."

"Arc-what-now?"

"Arcturus of the Boötes constellation, the brightest star in the northern celestial hemisphere, located approximately thirty-six light years from Earth."

"Oh, that Arcturus."

"You make me smile."

She raises her hand and orders two drinks.

"Caipirinha is our national cocktail, made with cachaça, sugar and lime."

"I'm not thirsty."

"They're both for me."

I throw my head back and laugh.

"My story is not that aberrant."

The waiter arrives with the cocktails.

"I'm all ears. Catch me up."

For the next two hours, I regale her with details of Cronus the Time Lord, Mani, the Temple of Arcturus, 5D, the related events on Earth, Ra, Baset, the gods of light, the Star Child and the Guardian of the Earth.

She hangs on every word. Asks numerous questions.

At midnight we walk back to the hotel. Her eyes are glazed.

I guess it's a lot of information to digest.

We clamber onto the bed for a cuddle.

She falls asleep quickly in my arms.

Kiss her gently on the forehead.

"Sweetest dreams, meu amor."

* * *

In the morning she is up bright and early.

Squint across the room at her.

"Eva, what's going on?"

"I'm packing."

"Really? Now?"

"It takes me a while."

I groan and pull the duvet over my head.

An hour later the aroma of fresh coffee wafts under my nose.

Blink and open my eyes.

"Morning, sleepyhead."

"Hey … Is that for me?"

"Yes. And that's all you're getting."

"Huh?"

"I'm still packing."

Ruffle my hair and sit up. Everything is blurry.

Hope she is not an early bird. I need my sleep.

Five minutes later a pair of socks is hurled at me.

"I'm excited. Are you going to shower?"

Slowly exhale.

"Alright."

Take a break from shaving. Sensitive skin.

I'm done in ten minutes. Hang the towel on the rail.

"Breakfast is ready. Shall we eat on the terrace?"

"Sure."

Thank goodness the coffee has kicked in.

Scrambled eggs and toasted bread rolls. Delicious blend of açaí, papaya and guaraná.

"I am becoming addicted to these smoothies."

She smiles amiably.

"We're still going to visit Ra today?"

"Uh huh."

"With all the talk last night, you never did explain the travel arrangements."

My hand brushes my necklace.

I pluck the Loophole and cast it to the ground.

"Think of your favourite spot on Ipanema beach. Somewhere you have been before."

"Okay."

"Now step through the portal."

"Are you sure?"

"Trust me."

She jumps and disappears.

Perfect. Peace and quiet. Now to settle down to breakfast.

Pour myself a steaming coffee. Turn on the lume. Watch the newsfeed.

Half an hour later she bursts through the door.

"That was incredible."

"Yep."

"You more awake now?"

"Uh huh."

"Can we leave soon?"

"Alright."

Turn off the lume, use the washroom, pack my suitcase.

"Ready when you are."

"I still need forty-five minutes."

Nothing I can do but smile.

"What's so amusing?"

"Something I saw on the newsfeed."

An hour later we are standing before the Loophole.

"You jump first, Eva. I'll throw the bags in after you. Then I'll follow."

"How long will the portal stay open?"

"Five seconds."

"That's not enough time."

"Hence, the Bell in my hand."

"What does that do?"

"The Bell slows everything except the Bell-ringer. It gives me a time advantage of thirty seconds."

"These sacred relics are amazing."

"They are indeed. Are you going to jump now?"

She gives me an earnest look and a deep kiss.

"See you on the other side."

Count three seconds. Ring the Bell. Throw the bags. Glance at the rippling ocean. Deep breath. Make the leap. Orchids swaying in the breeze.

"Where were you? I was worried."

"Right here, sweetheart."

"This is all new to me."

"Yeah. That's true."

Wrap my arms around her.

"Can't wait to see the ruins of Machu Picchu."

"Let's get settled first. I still have a room at the Sanctuary Lodge."

As we walk toward the hotel, greetings and hugs abound from various beings.

"Sat Sri Akal!"

"Greetings, Adam!"

"As-Salamu Alaykum!"

"Aisatsu!"

"Sanibonani!"

"Peace be upon you!"

"Um waynuma?"

"Rimaykullayki!"

She looks at me quizzically.

"You seem quite popular."

"No more than you, my darling."

We drop the luggage in my room. The window presents a splendid view of the mountain so we sit and enjoy it for a while.

"You going to show me around?"

"Sure. Let's go."

We stroll along the entrance path, choose the left trail and zigzag up the meandering steps. This takes us to the best vantage point. The time-worn ruins look mysterious and spectacular in the soft morning light. Magnificent mountain heads guard the sacred expanse of stone buildings.

"Wow, Adam. It's another world."

I stand behind her and slip my arms around her waist.

"Love you, my kindred spirit."

She nuzzles her cheek against mine.

"Love you too."

Far below, near the Temple of the Sun, is the solitary tree that bore witness to the ceremony of the summer solstice. It was the first time I met all the gods of light.

A small animal suddenly blurs through the air. Ferocious high-pitched screech.

Stephen Shaw

I jump with fright.

Eva seems relaxed and unfazed.

Moments later a sleek bronze Egyptian Mau is purring beside me.

"Baset! How lovely to see you."

She shifts to her less-favoured form: Tefnut, goddess of light.

Should have seen your face. It was hilarious.

"You always were a hyperactive cat."

Except when I'm not.

"I believe you have met my partner?"

Indeed.

She steps forward and embraces Eva.

Good to see you again. Well done on completing your mission.

"Thank you."

I notice the bristling energy. Eva is a passionate heart-centred woman. Honesty, integrity and direct communication are embedded in her core. She is the kind of person who will not easily forgive deceit or betrayal.

My mind flashes back to Africa. When Śakra reunited with Ra. The Star Child was furious with the sun-god, and the latter displayed seeming arrogance. Never apologised for not returning to save the Guardian of the Earth.

That is the difficulty with the gods of light. They have millennia of experience and vast knowledge. They have a far higher perspective than us mere humans. When they choose to withhold or partially share information, it is usually for a good reason. However, such behaviour can appear arrogant and uncaring.

Tefnut beckons Eva to sit with her on the grass step.

I loiter in the background while they chat.

Her hand gently touches Eva's shoulder.

Sorry I could not reveal my true identity back then. It would have put your life in danger.

Staring at the ground.

"How? Why?"

Do you know how you got to this point?

Silence.

We had our eye on you for a while. You have an interesting spirit.

Nonchalant shrug.

Let's recap. You were born in 1998. Attended university in 2016 at age 18; commenced a B.A. majoring in sociology and political science. In your first year you attended a lecture about ecology given by an external speaker. Remember?

"Uh huh."

I have to smile at Eva's petulance.

What was the speaker's name?

"I don't know. Maya something."

Indeed. Maya, also known as the Guardian of the Earth. A powerful Watcher.

My interjection bursts forth.

"The Guardian of the Earth? Lover of Star Child?"

She turns and gazes at me.

Maya was the soul mate and kindred spirit of Śakra.

"Kindred spirit?"

Tefnut gives me a disdainful look. I decide to keep quiet.

Eva tilts her head.

"What is a Watcher?"

Didn't Adam explain it to you?

"Not really."

I shift uncomfortably.

Before the gods left Earth approximately 2,000 years ago, we procreated two children of light. They were directed to stay on this planet until our return. Their mission was to watch over humankind, intervening only when absolutely necessary. They worked quietly and in secret, keeping a close eye on the natural world, genetic codes, advancing technology and politico-socio-economic systems.

"Understood."

You had a long discussion with Maya after the lecture.

"I did."

Recall the conversation?

Fervid nodding.

"Very inspirational. Motivated me toward political and social action."

She died in 2017 after battling Apophis.

"Oh ... The same Apophis that Adam defeated?"

The very one.

Eva glances at me with newfound respect. I feel redeemed.

Then you and I met in 2025.

"Yes. Your distinct appearance and zealous ideas were hard to miss."

We started the ball rolling on your social campaigns.

"I felt close to you. Then you left without saying a word."

Not before giving you Maya's time-dilation ring.

"This ring belonged to the Guardian of the Earth?"

It belonged to her on Arcturus before she became a Watcher.

"Wow. Everything is interconnected."

Welcome to the higher realities.

"Why didn't you tell me?"

If the Guardian or I had revealed our true identities, you would have been placed in grave danger. Apophis would have taken an interest in you.

"Oh."

Long pause.

"I didn't realise."

Tefnut raises her voice.

So you, Adam, were mentored by the Star Child and to some extent by Ra. And you, Eva, were inspired by the Guardian of the Earth and to some extent by me. You were each given at least one sacred object to protect your life.

I sit down next to Eva and hold her hand. It's all rather humbling when you are viewing things from a higher perspective. Reminds me of that hard but valuable lesson: Surrender and flow.

You need to remember there is a higher-order intelligence at work. It is never just your intentions. As you move deeper into integrity, impeccability and love, and align with the beings of light in higher dimensions, you will naturally enter a flow of cosmic order, of universal rhythm, a confluence of enlightened intentions.

A voice behind me booms.

Adam!

What is it with gods? Śakra was the same. Dramatic entrances and exits. Barely any small talk.

"Hey, Ra. What's up?"

Adam Kadmon. Slayer of the Dark Lizard.

He strides over and gives me a hug. Gosh, that's a first. We must have bonded during the battle of Machu Picchu.

The glowing bald-headed man with luminous blue eyes scrutinises Eva.

And who might you be?

Unsure whether to bow or extend her hand, Eva hesitates and Ra steps in for another hug. Wow. Two for two. What's going on?

He ruffles her hair and laughs.

I know who you are. Welcome.

Contemplating the sun-god's anomalous behaviour.

"You seem in a good mood," I venture.

He looks at me scornfully.

Arcturus was saved by Indra and Maya. The Arcturian Galactic Government regained stewardship of the galaxy. The gods, the humans and the Council of Light shattered the dark lattice that imprisoned Earth. You defeated the Dark Lizard. Śakra joined his true love in a higher dimension. There is much to celebrate.

For a brief moment I am confused. Oh yeah ... the Star Child's first name is Indra ... his second name is Śakra ... he insisted on being known by his second name when he left Arcturus to become a Watcher on Earth.

Perhaps these last few years have instilled a seriousness in me. Constant skirmishes with dark ones. Ever-changing mentors and geographic locations. No place to call home. Surrendering, growing, learning, flowing.

Śakra once described me as *'sensitive, moody and task-oriented.'*

A smile lights up my face. It's probably true.

"Touché. Much to celebrate."

I notice Tefnut has reverted to Baset the Egyptian Mau. She is purring and winding herself around the sun-god's legs.

Ra slides his arm across my shoulders.

Come on, Adam. Let's walk down to the solstice tree. We have much to discuss.

Baset stares at Eva and miaows coquettishly. Even I cannot interpret the signal.

She is asking if you'd like a tour of the ruins.

Clapping her hands. "Yes, please."

I glance at Eva and smile. Both of our moods have shifted. We have acclimatised to the brusque sagacious gods. I wonder what our time on this mountain will bring.

* * *

I am sitting with Ra beneath the solstice tree. It is warm and sunny. Surveying the stone ruins and verdant steps. Machu Picchu is a lush and magical place. Not just the harbinger of mysterious memories but a repository of potent energies.

Let's talk about your destiny.

"Straight to business."

Indeed, Adam.

"Alright."

It's time to fulfil your mission.

"Rebuild this world."

More than rebuild. Create a new way of life.

"Meaning?"

Antiquated ideologies and systems must retire.

"Political, economic, social?"

Everything. The dark lattice has been broken. Humans are now completely self-responsible. The old ways of political and economic control being concentrated in the hands of a powerful few ... sham democracies creating the illusion of freedom ... governments being run by corporations and corporate lobbyists ... the destruction of rainforests and other precious natural resources ... the vast swathes of poor and starving people ...

"It must end."

You need revolution not evolution.

"Aha."

The world is looking for new leaders. Apophis impressed then betrayed entire nations. Large shoes are waiting to be filled. Existence of gods and higher dimensions have been revealed. The world is ready for dramatic change.

I heave a deep sigh.

"What do you want me to do?"

This planet needs spiritual leadership first and foremost. It needs leaders who display and live integrity, impeccability and love. Leaders who truly care about people and planet.

"Who are these leaders?"

The sun-god stares at me.

"Oh ..."

Hope these last seven years have not been wasted on you.

Ouch.

"Any advice?"

Close your eyes. Sense the higher energies.

I do so. At once a vision rushes into my consciousness. Eva and I holding hands, standing at the top of a huge pyramid. Just below us the Council of Light, encircling the apex of the pyramid, clasping each other's wrists, singing, chanting, praying, meditating. Below them a band of learned individuals, experts in various fields, proffering knowledge, debating, implementing. Layers and layers of beings descending all the way down to the base of the pyramid.

I notice a brilliant light hovering in the heavens. It bursts into a cascade of flickering stars, rippling through individuals ... communities ... nations. Glorious celestial music ... every being reaching to the ones below ... beckoning, supporting, encouraging ... flowing waves of kindness ... a cosmic dance of love.

You understand now?

"Uh huh."

Tell me.

"Loving-kindness, impeccability and application of advanced knowledge."

That will do for now.

"Anything else?"

Ra reaches into his pocket then displays his upturned palm. I lean forward and scrutinise the tiny luminescent bubble. It's about the size of a pea, semi-translucent, with a glimmering mother-of-pearl sheen.

"Beautiful. What is it?"

It comes from my home world. It's a gift and responsibility.

He hands it to me.

I swallow cautiously.

"What do I do with it?"

Add it to your necklace for a start.

The sun-god points the Staff of Light at the bubble.

You now have sole dominion over it.

"Are you going to explain this sacred object?"

We have guided and mentored you for seven years. Everything you have learned needs to be applied now. The gods promised to help rebuild your world while ensuring that power and governance remain firmly in the hands of humans. Over to you. It's in your hands.

"What about this object?"

Only you can decide the object's dimensions and what will be inside.

"Could you be a little more vague?"

Ra stands up, squeezes my shoulder and smiles.

You and Eva will work it out. Have a short vacation. The world is waiting for you.

I lean back against the tree and watch him walk away.

It's been like this throughout the last seven years. Always trying to catch up with the gods and the spiritual mentors. Their obscure and abstruse lessons. Just enough to lure my inquisitive nature; yet never enough to let me indulgently wallow.

I know why the gods never spoon-feed knowledge. You have to wrestle with it, absorb it, apply it. The central tenet is always *self-responsibility, self-empowerment, self-determination.* The gods refuse to create dependent vacuous followers.

I shake my head and grin. You cannot escape responsibility. No one is going to live your life for you. The secret is to learn to work together. To move your own life forward, assist others to move their lives forward, and ask others to help you.

Self-responsibility and shared responsibility.

In the distance I notice Eva and Tefnut engaged in animated conversation. Glad to see they are getting along. I wonder what they are discussing. Is Eva receiving similar guidance?

We meet later in the hotel garden. The sun is gently disappearing below the horizon. A soft breeze is fluttering the orchids. Birds are murmuring and nuzzling in the trees. Dinner is outside on the terrace. It's ceviche, a delicious mixture of raw fish, lime juice, chopped onion and chilli.

The sky transitions from day to night. A full moon rises mystically and splashes silver across the stone ruins. I am gazing into her beautiful eyes. The atmosphere is serene and reflective.

* * *

In the morning she is up early again.

I throw a pillow at her in mock anger.

"You can't be serious!"

"What?"

"Bring that luscious body over here."

"Hmm?"

I smile mischievously.

"You need a cuddle."

She acquiesces and leaps onto the bed.

"Gently now. I have just woken."

A sultry wink. Flicks her long auburn hair.

"Alright. Just stay on your back."

She straddles my hips, leans forward and kisses me sensuously.

"Mmm … you smell good."

"And you need a shave."

"Bit rough?"

She nods, slips me inside her.

Sexy cadence … staring into each other's eyes …

Surrendering to the luscious rhythm …

Exquisite unruffled energy …

Her eyes close.

My heart suddenly gasps with love.

"Eva, what's happening?"

"You are touching Tantra, dear soul."

"Huh?"

Her voice has become ethereal.

"You have forgotten what Śakra taught you?"

What a time to use my brain.

"Uh … 'The journey of Tantra is the wildest exposure of one's own heart and the most loving acceptance of another's heart.'"

"Exactly."

She slows her rhythm, then stops.

I frown.

"And now?"

"The orgasm you know is called a *peak orgasm*. It is the chase of lust and biological drive ending in release and ejaculation."

"Yeah, I really like that."

"If you remain still inside me and focus your attention on the energies flowing between us, you may encounter a *valley orgasm*. This requires no movement; merely an increased awareness."

"You mean the energy flowing between our hearts?"

"Yes, my darling."

Great time for a lesson. Shouldn't have let her eyes close.

No choice really. Place my hand on my chest.

"You feel that?"

"Yes … the energy is increasing."

Rather peculiar.

"I can sense the vibration of our hearts. It's like a …"

"Tantric conversation?"

"Yeah, I guess."

Fervent, cascading back and forth.

"Oh … oh … oh my …"

I hear her pleasurable utterances too.

Suddenly I am orgasming in my heart.

Shouting with euphoria … weeping with joy …

"Oh, Eva!"

She lays on top of me and we disappear into cocooned ecstasy.

A few minutes later, I mumble my confusion.

"No ejaculation. And I feel energised."

"Physiological sex with genital orgasm is the lowest rung on the ladder. It is a relatively simple and boring pleasure."

"Oh. I was really enjoying it."

"You just experienced an orgasm in your heart chakra. Was that not enjoyable?"

"It was incredible and ecstatic. Wait a minute. Chakra?"

I reach to activate the lume. Eva will be dismayed if she misses this.

Deep sigh. She rolls over and lays next to me.

I prop myself on one elbow.

"Alright. I'm listening."

"Chakras are energy centres located in that transitory space between the soul and other-dimensional realities."

"Hmm ... explain further."

Another deep sigh.

"The name derives from the Sanskrit word for *wheel* or *turning*. In the Tantric and Yogic context, a better translation would be *vortex* or *whirlpool*."

Intuitive insight.

"You mean connectors ... transporters and translators of energy?"

"Yes. Try to imagine whirlpools connecting from highest dimensions, swirling down through various layers of reality, including the soul and physical world."

"You mean like the Vortex of Life?"

"Mmm ... like miniature versions ... so you can travel along aspects ... for example, physical heart ... heart chakra ... romantic love ... spiritual love ... divine love ... mystical love ... all the way to ultimate Love."

"Therefore you can raise the resonance of different aspects of yourself."

"Indeed. The chakras in each soul are connected by a central channel. Each wheel or vortex sits perpendicular to the channel, connecting outward to the ever-expanding ripples of that aspect."

"And that includes other souls."

"That is correct."

"So we can merge the energies of our chakras."

"Now you understand."

She giggles softly.

"Can you handle the next level?"

"Sure, why not?"

"Imagine the Source, unmanifested Consciousness, as an enormous Ocean spiralling down into innumerable creations. For a single creation, picture an enormous vortex rotating through various aspects of existence down to a single point – a base or root chakra. The essence of that particular creation lies coiled in the root chakra."

"Wow, that's deep."

"Unfortunately, many teachers have corrupted Tantra and reduced it to sex, pleasure and sensuality."

"What is it supposed to be?"

"A path to awakening."

"Aha."

"True Tantra explores the way of the chakras. Each level of Tantra corresponds to a particular chakra, starting with the base or root chakra (Muladhara – *root support*), then sacral chakra (Svadhishthana – *one's own base*), then solar plexus chakra (Manipura – *jewel city*), then heart chakra (Anahata – *pristine*), then throat chakra (Vishuddha – *especially pure*), then third-eye chakra (Ajna – *command*), and finally crown chakra (Sahasrara – *thousand-petaled*)."

She place her fingertips on each chakra as she is explaining.

"Tantra is the journey shared by kindred spirits on the way to the Light. Most souls merely taste Tantra. Only kindred spirits immerse into Tantra."

"Why?"

"Commitment to each other and the dream-cycle of Love. Prerequisites for the path of Tantra."

"I understand."

"To facilitate a chakra orgasm or multiple-chakra orgasm, you can utter the sacred mantra 'Hari Om'. 'Hari' initiates the removal of low-vibration energy and is therefore a healing word. 'Om' invites the Light, thereby shifting the resonance of the chakra toward the Source. Preferably pronounce it 'Aum' as this is the primordial sound."

"A chakra orgasm can take place within an individual and as a shared experience with another being?"

"Correct."

"So much to learn."

"Those who follow the path are called Tantrikas."

"I prefer being called a kindred spirit."

Her eyes flutter open.

"Hey … what happened?"

"You closed your eyes and delivered a lecture."

"In the middle of …"

"Yeah."

"I'm still so wet."

Nonchalant shrug.

"Ready if you are."

She straddles my hips.

Surrendering to the luscious rhythm …

I smile to myself. A chakra orgasm can wait.

Oh my …

* * *

We spend the next few days exploring the mystical ruins, making delicious love, and enjoying mouth-watering food on the sunlit terrace. How wonderful to have a best friend, lover and romantic partner in one person. I am engulfed in joy.

Ra and Tefnut seem to be leaving us alone. Perhaps this time is a respite from the impending pressures. After all, we are supposed to become leaders of the world.

Rubbing my eyebrow.

"I feel a bit apprehensive."

"Why?"

"This huge mission before us."

"We'll be alright."

"I have no idea how to proceed."

"That bubble must have something to do with it."

I touch my necklace.

"Yeah."

She gives me a close embrace.

"I love you, Adam. We'll work it out together."

"That's what Ra said."

"Give me the bubble."

I place it in her hand.

"Should we give it a proper name?"

"How much did Ra explain?"

"As little as possible."

Her brow creases.

"Let's call it the Bubble. It is a sacred object."

"Alright."

"Show me what it can do."

"Place it on the ground."

I order the Bubble to expand to a three-metre cube.

Eva looks at me avidly.

"Can I peek inside?"

I invoke that our energy resonances can enter.

"Give it a go."

She sticks her head through the sheen.

A moment later, gasping, "There's no air. And it's dark."

"Oh. Right."

I command that suitable breathing air and light permeate the cube.

"Try again?"

Tentative survey. She steps inside.

I follow her through the rippling wall.

"Wow, this is crazy!"

"I know. Nothing but light and air."

"Hey, you're naked."

"You too."

"What happened to our clothes?"

I glimpse through the shimmering barrier.

"Still outside. I only permitted our resonances to enter."

"You can control what enters?"

"Yep."

"Purrfect."

"Hmm?"

"Adam, this is it. This is how we do it."

"What?"

"Create a whole new world."

"Not sure I understand."

She strokes her lip thoughtfully.

"We need to choose a state in North America."

Glance at her quizzically.

"And build a model world."

"How?"

"You control the Bubble. I have this gift of Knowledge."

"We build everything from scratch?"

"With the help of experts."

"Daunting responsibility."

She frowns, exhales softly.

"The last few years have primed us for this task. We can do it."

Nod my head pensively.

"I want to make Śakra proud."

"I owe it to the women and children of this planet."

We hold hands and stare at the brooding mountain heads. A silver moon is bathing the enigmatic ruins, creating an inscrutable interplay of gleaming illumination and oblique shadows.

There is a big journey ahead of us.

* * *

Laying on the bed with Eva, staring out the window ... glorious viridescent nature and cheerful tweeting of birds ... mmm ... this will be an essential part of our new world. I draw her in for a cuddle ... caressing her soft face ... gazing into radiant blue eyes ... heart leaps ... truly windows to the soul ... conveying exquisite love ...

"Sweetheart ..."

"Meu amor ..."

"I was wondering ..."

"Hmm?"

"Before this huge mission starts, can we explore your gift?"

"As long as you always record the lesson."

"Of course."

"You in the mood now?"

"Sure."

I activate the lume.

Her eyes close.

"Please will you expatiate on Tantra."

She giggles.

"Esoteric or vanilla flavour?"

Makes me smile.

Stephen Shaw

"Uh ... vanilla flavour."

The characteristic deep sigh.

"Tantrikas keenly respect the human body, regarding it as a holy temple of the soul. There is, at minimum, a fastidious focus on optimal nutrition and avoidance of pollutants."

"Interesting."

"Making love is sacred to Tantrikas. As such, it is boundaried in a loving committed partnership. Sex is not shared beyond the romantic relationship. Pornography is eschewed."

I raise my eyebrows.

"Tantrikas use these sacred labels: Penis is called *lingam* (wand of light); scrotum and testicles are called *devamani* (divine jewels); vulva and vagina are called *yoni* (sacred space); clitoris is called *clio*; anus is called *rosetta* (tiny rose)."

"Respect and reverence."

"Precisely."

"*Foreplay* is a redundant word in Tantra, as there are no stages or goals. Tantrikas prefer the term *loveplay* or *lila* which is any kind of intimate, affectionate, sexual frolicking as an end in itself."

I cough quietly.

"Can we shift attention to esoteric Tantra?"

Long moment of silence.

"The secret of Kundalini."

"Kunda-what-now?"

"Do you remember the previous teaching?"

"Um … Source … chakras …?"

"Imagine the Source, unmanifested Consciousness, as an enormous Ocean spiralling down into innumerable creations. For a single creation, picture an enormous vortex rotating through various aspects of existence down to a single point – a base or root chakra. The essence of that particular creation lies coiled in the root chakra."

"Ah, yes."

"Kundalini or *coiled* energy is represented as a sleeping serpent residing in the root chakra. When the serpent awakens, it uncoils and extends up the central channel or *sushumna nadi*, through every chakra until it reaches the crown chakra. The serpent carries the consciousness of every chakra along to all the subsequent chakras, resulting in profound insights, overpowering visions, ecstatic states and orgasmic enlightenment."

"Wow."

"Powerful consciousness-shifting practices should only be done under the mentorship of an experienced guru, yogi or spiritual master."

"Why?"

"Any venture into other-dimensional realities and heightened-awareness states requires hand-holding and perspicacious guidance. You do not want to risk a psychotic break or negative episode."

"Understood."

"Do you recall what Sikh Nanak taught you about Shakti?"

"That was many years ago."

"He said 'There exists nothing but God and his Shakti. God is the unmanifested observer and she is the embodiment of his dreams. She creates all the universes with her endless love. She in fact *is* the creation. All of creation is merely a beautiful cloak to wrap God in and make him visible.'"

"Oh yeah ... a beautiful aphorism."

"Kundalini can also be envisaged as the goddess Shakti. When the sleeping goddess awakens, she travels through the various layers of reality or chakras and reunites with Shiva, resulting in the ultimate Tantric union. That is the In-Breath taught by Ra."

I recite the teaching. "'*The Source manifests countless dimensions and infinite realities – the Out-Breath, the act of creation. And all of creation flows back to the Source – the In-Breath, the return and dissolution. This is the flow of Life.*'"

She beams a huge smile.

"Exactly."

"Tantra is a path to awakening."

Eva nods contentedly.

"That's enough for today."

Her eyelids flutter.

Gazing into her gorgeous blue eyes.

Enfold her gently in my arms.

"I love you, precious person."

"I love you, meu amor."

"You feel like going for a walk?"

"Thought you'd never ask."

"All the information is stored in the lume. Plenty of time to assimilate it."

"Purrfection."

We bound off the bed, enjoy a long shower together, get cosily dressed and head out the door.

* * *

"What's the name of the state?"

I am happily munching scrambled eggs, soft toast and creamy avocado.

"Which state?"

"Exactly."

"Oh. To set up base."

She nods fervidly.

"I think we should choose one that is struggling economically."

Activate the lume and instruct a search.

Instant response: 'The ten poorest states are Mississippi, West Virginia, Alabama, South Carolina, New Mexico, Kentucky, Idaho, Arkansas, Montana, Maine.'

"Display map."

A colourful hologram pops up.

"Aha. These states are geographically close: South Carolina, Alabama, Mississippi, Arkansas. Kentucky and West Virginia are just north."

She peruses the map.

"Mississippi."

"I'll ask Ra to get us an audience with the president."

"He can do that?"

"We saved the world."

"True."

I study the orchids fluttering on the terrace.

As if reading our minds, the sun-god appears with Baset.

Sits down at the breakfast table.

You two ready now?

I glance at Eva. She nods.

The Staff of Light is a marvellous sacred object which interfaces with every communication system on Earth. Soon Ra has set up the appointment.

"Are we doing a personal visit or an interactive hologram?"

The latter. Tomorrow morning. After that, you need to move.

Noticing the subtle urgency in his voice.

I guess the vacation is over.

Reaching for Eva's hand.

"Let's take a last ramble through this mysterious place."

"And prepare what we want to say."

"Yeah. A decent proposal."

She giggles uneasily.

The rest of the day flutters by. I have moments of apprehension and mild anxiety. We hold hands and discuss our vision and strategy. There is so much we don't know. Few exemplars exist for this situation. All we can do is promote the potential benefits for humankind.

In the morning Ra invites us to an empty meeting room. We trade a few words, take a deep breath, then activate the hologram.

The president is unexpectedly receptive to our ideas. When resistance arises, Ra takes a firm position. Our proposal is formidable and daunting. We want carte blanche in the state of Mississippi. The progress of our manufactured world will be showcased to the entire planet. Everyone will be watching.

I realise after the meeting that humans are still reeling at the revelation of gods, extraterrestrials, reverse engineering, Area 51, Apophis and the dark forces. People are amenable and ready for constructive and beneficial change.

Within a few hours Ra and the president appear on the newsfeed. After a general announcement and placation from the president, Ra takes over in his usual dramatic and bold fashion, reiterating the assistance of the gods and the promise of power and governance remaining firmly in the hands of humans.

His final statement is uplifting and inspiring: *It is the dawn of the Golden Age on Earth.*

As for Eva and I, we are packing our bags hurriedly. We have a flight to catch and a new world to create.

* * *

Our mission begins.

The government has assigned an area of 1,000 square kilometres for our project. A bleak geographical landscape devastated by Apophis. Nothing here but scorched earth. It's perfect.

We have supplies for one month, so time is of the essence. As soon as the helicopter flies away, we get to work.

Put the bags down, cast the miniaturised Bubble to the ground, command its expansion to 1,000 square kilometres, then invoke a height of 2,500 metres to avoid all commercial jetliners and general aviation craft.

"Adam, I would like to suggest a name for our world."

"Go ahead."

"Eden."

Broad smile.

"So be it."

Grab an apple from the basket and begin munching.

"Would you like a bite?"

"Love one."

"Right. Where do we start?"

"How about I close my eyes and impart vital knowledge?"

"Hmm. First we need AI machines and 3D printers."

"AI?"

"Artificial Intelligence with closed learning loops."

"So we stay in control."

"Exactly."

I tap the Adi Shakti and spend ten minutes conversing with Ra.

Eva is scrutinising my necklace.

"Meu amor, what is that device?"

"A sacred object for advanced communication and protection."

"Aha."

"While we are waiting for the machines to be delivered …"

She lays down. Her eyes flicker.

For the next three hours I am regaled with countless concepts, designs and specifications.

Eva finally rouses and sits up.

"All good?"

"Excellent, my darling."

"Captured all the information?"

I brush my fingers across the lume and smile.

The AI machines arrive the next day. Nine colossal multi-limbed constructors. And a silver-blue humanoid master which we activate immediately.

My name is Anunaki. How may I serve you, Adam and Eva?

I interface the lume and download the data.

My hands move to the prayer position.

Eva wraps her arm around my waist.

I gaze into her excited sapphire eyes.

"Ready to create a new world?"

She blinks a few times.

"Let's do it."

Solemn countenance.

"Anunaki, adapt the 3D printers to utilise cosmic energy."

According to the blueprint?

"Yes."

Scratching my chin.

"Then build us a home. Two people."

Proceeding.

We watch in fascination as specialised AI machines construct the first building.

Eva glances at me.

"What is cosmic energy?"

"Free energy. Cosmic energy is captured to generate power *and* cosmic energy is transmuted directly into matter. Advanced science delivered by you, my darling."

"Beyond solar, geothermal, wind and wave energy?"

"Absolutely."

"Zero cost, zero emission, zero pollution?"

"Indeed."

Our new home is complete within hours. We begin exploring the circular building. The design is like a doughnut with all rooms facing a beautiful internal courtyard which is covered by a weather-sensitive retractable roof in the form of spiralling flower petals. Inspired by Mediterranean culture, all external walls are permanently white. Inner walls and ceilings vary from transparent to opaque to multi-coloured depending on voice or touch command. Each wall is also a lume, displaying television, newsfeed, communication, games, videos, photos or digital art, contingent on user preference.

To the right of the entrance hall is a spacious family room then dining room then a relatively small kitchen. Eva looks disappointed.

I consult the wall lume.

The eye-level device is a food replicator which creates meals and drinks directly from energy. It responds to touch or voice command. Select from 100 recipes. The trash bin at floor level reverses the process. The bin will not activate until the lid is closed. Safety precautions have been installed. The mid-level device is for cleaning crockery, cutlery, glassware, etc. It washes, disinfects and dries; no water required. Next to that unit is a larger machine for washing, disinfecting and drying clothes. The kitchen is self-cleaning and remains germ-free.

"No wonder it is so tiny."

She brushes her hand along the cupboards at each side, then peruses the marblesque work-surface beneath.

"Very attractive design. Highly functional. I like it."

"Best part is no cooking, no cleaning, no trash."

"We'll need more recipes though."

She makes a note in her lume.

We stroll across the courtyard and enter the main bedroom. Replete with wardrobes, wingback chairs and small table. A shimmering king-size bed projects from the external wall. We clamber aboard. A benign voice enquires *May we establish settings?*

Eva waves her fingers. "Make it so."

We are gently levitating on an energy field. There is no limb compression. Our postures are subtly adjusted to optimise comfort and orthopaedic health. It is extraordinarily relaxing. Ambient sound, lighting and temperature are monitored and maintained within requested parameters. When not in sleep mode, it functions as a massage and healing bed, offering various therapeutic treatments.

Eva sighs happily.

"I can't wait to have a massage."

"We'll never leave the house again."

"And no bedding, no pillows. No washing."

"Mmm ..."

She grabs my hand.

"Let's check out the washroom."

Immaculate. Floor-to-ceiling curved mirrored cabinet. Huge waterless shower. Pristine lavatory.

"Wha-a-a-t?"

I consult the wall lume.

The shower illumines the body with radiant energy. Cleans and disinfects and dries. No water required. All bathroom waste products are safely and automatically converted to energy. For haircut and styling, please sit in front of the mirror and select one of the 20 options. For permanent or temporary body hair removal, please stand in front of the mirror and specify the area. The washroom is self-cleaning and remains germ-free.

Eva ruffles her long auburn hair.

"20 options? That's going to require an upgrade."

She makes another note in her lume.

Resting my hands on my hips.

The building design is ingenious. Front door and entrance hall. Family, dining and kitchen located on right side of the 'doughnut'; guest lavatory, bedroom, washroom and office located on left side. All rooms have access to the inner courtyard. Each room also has internal access to adjoining rooms.

I tap the wall lume.

"Tell me about safety and security."

The home is constantly monitored to ensure an optimal and safe environment. Everything is fire-proof and weather-proof. Emergency protocols and procedures are in place. Access to the home is granted via voice or facial recognition. There is unremitting communication between the home and the individual's personal lume.

"Impressive."

Eva tilts her head. Her brow furrows.

"Every person should have a home like this. Security, space, comfort, nutritious food, zero running costs. Activities can then be focused on the well-being and pleasure of society, instead of survival and competition."

I rub her lower back affectionately.

"That's why I love you, my darling."

"We are going to need some experts."

"Probably."

"More recipes for a start."

"Indeed."

"So, what's next?"

"How about a delightful massage?"

"Best idea of the day."

We amble across to the expansive bed.

"I wonder if it has a hot tub setting."

She raises an eyebrow and smiles.

We clamber aboard and select individual massages.

Eva places her hand upon mine.

"See you on the other side, my love."

Already drifting away ... murmur an endearment ... surrender into bliss ...

* * *

In the morning she bounces out of bed.

Returns with a tray of croissants, steaming cappuccino and pingado.

"The food replicator is amazing. Three minutes. Taste a croissant."

I sit up and the energy field immediately supports my back. Can it get any more comfortable than this?

Rub my eyes.

"Best sleep of my life."

She sets the tray upon my lap. I slip my hands around the caramel-coloured mug.

"Wow. That's a good cappuccino."

"Mmm. Taste a croissant."

Flaky, soft, buttery.

"Divine."

"This is so exciting. No shopping, cooking, cleaning or washing. Just living, loving and being!"

Her morning enthusiasm is contagious. Soon we are discussing the next phase of Eden's development. We sketch out ideas on the wall lume.

"Let's build cities in the form of a spiral or vortex. At the centre of the vortex will be an Assembly Chamber for city meetings ... Hall of Learning ... Medical Services ... Entertainment Multiplex with auditoriums, concert halls, cinemas, theatres, art galleries, museums."

"Homes will spiral away from the centre ... with parks, playgrounds and recreation areas interspersed between the arms of the spiral ... sports fields and training facilities located toward the outer arms of the spiral."

"We can build temples beyond the outermost spiral ... away from homes and other buildings ... where it is quietest and surrounded by nature."

I study the design layout.

"Imagine a bicycle wheel superimposed upon the spiral ... the spokes represent straight avenues of travel from city centre to outer limits ... with concentric ring roads intersecting the avenues ... automated vehicles will transport people along these avenues and roads ..."

Eva is stroking her lip.

"Why do homes have to be on the ground? There are 5.5 billion people on this planet. What if homes are clustered into colossal AI trees ... and the trees are built on the spiral?"

Scratching my head.

"The trunk of the tree could contain a huge elevator ... and homes would be built along circular horizontal ascending branches ... ensuring unobstructed panoramic views for all occupants ... the branches could be enclosed motorised walkways ... with spokes connecting the circular branches to the central trunk."

"Do you realise that all buildings and constructions are spherical or rounded ... everything is built on spirals ... with connecting spokes?"

"Yeah … I like it."

"Me too."

"Can we make all buildings white? Matt white with minimal reflective sheen. It will inspire feelings of purity and cleanliness. Be wonderful against the verdant greenery in which our cities will be immersed. It will also reduce comparison and competitiveness."

"Makes a lot of sense. Anyway, people can decorate and customise the inside of their homes and courtyards as they wish."

"One more thing. Let's make our home the standard unit. Homes should have the capacity to expand and create additional rooms relative to family size. This can be an automated process."

We summon Anunaki.

How may I serve you, Adam and Eva?

"Cross-reference all previously uploaded data and search best practices from around the planet. Construct a city within these newly-defined parameters."

Searching. Uploading to AI machines and 3D printers. Proceeding.

In three months, under Anunaki's directives, a beautiful city is built over an area of 60 square kilometres. After a thorough inspection, we make minor amendments to the blueprints and instruct the building of more cities. Each city will be located 40 kilometres from its neighbour in a vast grid formation, spanning the entire allotted 1,000 square kilometres. In total, therefore, 100 cities will be constructed.

A few weeks later Eva and I are strolling through the bleak landscape. She seems unsettled.

"I have a jumble of thoughts and feelings."

"Share with me."

"Although the construction is spectacular, there is still no nature. We need to import experts in natural sciences and landscaping."

"Okay."

"We also need to invite the president and world leaders to survey our work."

"Uh huh."

"I don't want the purity of our world corrupted."

"You think we need a manifesto?"

"Manifesto?"

"A public declaration of policy and aims. Living and operating principles. Entrance requirements for Eden."

A glimmer of excitement.

"That's a great idea."

"We could paste it electronically every 100 metres on the Bubble's external wall. Along with cautions and expectations."

"Purrfect."

"Anything else?"

"Yes. We are going to need some clothes."

"Ah. Good point."

We consult with Anunaki.

Recommendation: Nanotech fibre. As light and smooth as satin, breathable, durable, waterproof, temperature-regulated, bacteria-phobic, virus-phobic, impenetrable to projectiles, self-cleaning. Nanofibres harmlessly conduct cosmic energy, enabling clothing to shift colour and pattern as instructed. Liquid crystallinity effectively results in a wearable lume, allowing instant communication with other lumes.

Eva smiles broadly.

"Upload data to the 3D printer in our home office."

Done. Design requirements?

She glances at me.

"What should we do? Uniforms are abhorrent, yet we need a world without social comparison and competition. Where people are valued for who they are, not for what they wear."

"Personally I could wear the same thing every day, especially if those nanofibres can change colour and pattern."

Her brow creases.

"So much social and gender conditioning to overcome."

"Um ... create one style of each of the following ... knee-length and full-length skirt ... knee-length and full-length dress ... collared blouse ... plain trousers ... cargo trousers ... collared shirt ... shorts ... t-shirt ... boxers ... briefs ... hipster ... bikini ... socks ... sandals ... comfortable shoes ... training shoes ... ankle boots ... long boots."

"Jackets, jerseys, scarves, hats?"

"Not necessary. Eden is temperature-regulated."

"Anything else?"

"Capuchin hooded robe. Assigned to each person on arrival, as they will be required to enter naked and with no possessions."

"That's going in the manifesto?"

"Absolutely."

"And no high heels."

"Sounds good to me."

She points a finger at Anunaki.

"Make it so."

Proceeding.

Place my arm across her shoulders.

"Let's go home. I want to print a psychedelic robe."

"Psychedelic?"

"Vibrant colours ... vermilion, gold, cyan ... maybe in stripes."

She looks at me and giggles.

"A customised hooded robe?"

I summon a taxi and smile.

"Yeah, why not?"

* * *

Six months later we invite the president of North America to tour Eden. After all, he is still leader of this continent. Receiving outsider feedback might also be invaluable to our direction and progress. Although we are downloading advanced knowledge via Eva, the truth is our perspective may be a little cloistered.

We have yet to design and display a manifesto. However, we have made it clear that whoever enters Eden will do so utterly naked. The Bubble will automatically cleanse individuals of harmful bacteria, viruses and germs upon entrance into our sacred world.

Access points have been designated every 100 kilometres along the border of Eden, numbered NE1 (north-east corner) to NE10 (running south to SE1) and so forth. The president and his entourage, which we have limited to ten people, will arrive at NE1.

As the visit approaches, our trepidation increases. Will we lose control of our sacred world? Will the president approve of our designs and ideas? Why do we care so much?

I have started to realise that Eden has become our child. It is a beautiful creation that we lovingly nurture and protect. We also sense the huge weight of responsibility because we are building a possible future for our planet.

The day finally arrives and we are waiting patiently at the north-east corner. Is being late a deliberate flexing of power? I hope not.

Politics and posturing will have no place in Eden.

After a tedious hour, two large black helicopters land outside the Bubble. Once the politicians disembark, we wave and point to the robes folded neatly on the table. We then step away and politely avert our eyes. I smile quietly. This ought to be interesting.

It takes thirty minutes of commotion and complaining but eventually the ever-so-slightly humbled leaders, and presumably a bodyguard or two, walk over and greet us.

We grin apprehensively and shake hands.

"Welcome to Eden. Hope it inspires and excites you."

The tour takes about three hours. The temples, sports fields, parks and playgrounds are not yet complete. There is no natural environment. However, the city centre appears to be "superb" and the communities-in-the-trees are "remarkable" and "awesome". The entire concept blows them away. A late lunch is produced quickly and easily from a food replicator, with individuals selecting from a newly extended menu. We reveal the city blueprints during dessert.

The critique is no surprise. "Stop doing it alone and bring in experts from various fields: politics, economics, engineering, landscaping, medical, education and entertainment." The president offers to leave two leaders to assist us. We adamantly refuse. Maybe this is viewed as obstinacy but it is unlikely they understand our vision of a new world.

The mention of economics irks me. Don't they understand? Everything is free in Eden. Energy, housing, food, clothes, medical, education, entertainment. What use is money and economics? And what of politics? Will it even have a role? Certainly not the usual style of politics, linked to the sham of democracy, vested financial interests and corporate lobbyists. Those days are over.

The 'old guard' leave as naked as they arrived. Perhaps there is a message in their departure. We collect the robes and wave a relieved goodbye. Never again. As Ra so eloquently put it: *'Antiquated ideologies and systems must retire.'*

The good news is we have received a wake-up call. We cannot do this alone. Much pondering and discussion lies ahead.

Now I need a long blissful shower. Eva needs a long blissful hug.

It's time to strategise and move forward.

* * *

We wake up bright-eyed and raring to go. The supreme quality of sleep every night coupled with our respective morning coffees only adds fuel to our emotional fire. We are eager to proceed to the next level.

Eva already has her list displayed on the lume:

Create a vast healthy menu to cater for diverse tastes.
Immerse our cities in nature. Aesthetic landscape design.
Locate experts for medical, education and entertainment.
Manifesto for entrance requirements and living principles.

I am looking over her shoulder, affectionately nuzzling her cheek.

"Let's do the Manifesto first. We'll need it prior to bringing people into Eden."

"Difficult one."

"Why?"

"We have to balance freedom and control."

"Meaning?"

"No one likes rules. Especially in paradise."

I bite my lip and frown.

"Do you think people can govern themselves?"

She quietly contemplates the issue.

"I guess the real question is human nature."

"Yeah."

"Are people naturally kind and altruistic or selfish and greedy?"

"Perhaps in an environment where all survival needs are met, kindness and service will flourish."

"I believe that will be true."

Staring out the window ... envisioning a verdant landscape.

"Being surrounded by lush nature will nourish the goodness in humans."

"Nature and beauty exhilarate the soul."

"What about harmful energy?"

She gives me a quizzical look.

"Emotional and psychological wounds ... abusive childhoods ... harsh backgrounds ... such people will bring negative energy into Eden ... no matter how beautiful it is here."

"We'll need healers and carers. Perhaps a transitory space for gradual integration into society. Places of deep compassion, kindness and wisdom. Either medical services or temples."

"There must be plenty of people who would love to do such work."

Rubbing my chin.

"And what about work? No one needs to earn money or pay for anything."

"It's connected to human nature again."

"How so?"

"People who have their survival needs met will naturally explore their creativity."

"Manifest their essences."

"Of course. Artists will write and paint. Musicians will create music. Athletes will do sport and dance. Intellectual people will study, research and teach. Scientists will explore. Those who love nature might volunteer in the parks. Entertainers will create films and theatrical events. Healers will work in medical services or the temples."

"Humans will inevitably serve society and the planet."

"Ideal living conditions and optimal environments encourage prosocial, altruistic and creative behaviour."

Solemnly nodding.

"I hope so."

Eva smiles at me.

"You know what this means, don't you?"

"No."

"We need to let go."

"Let go?"

"Share the reins. Surrender and trust."

"Leadership with a light touch."

"Exactly."

"Bring in the experts."

"Indeed."

"Let's have another coffee and churn ideas for a Manifesto."

"Only if you bring chocolate croissants."

"Deal. Back in a few minutes."

Hmm. Will paradise precipitate its own problems? Are humans ready for Utopia? Will they be able to handle free energy, housing, food, medical, education and entertainment? Will society be productive or bask in the sun all day? Will chaos and anarchy ensue? Will we take care of each other? Will love, compassion and kindness blossom? Time will reveal the truth.

Ah. Steaming tray of yumminess.

Eva hands me my favourite mug.

"New recipe. Hold onto your socks."

"Really? What is it?"

"Take a sip."

"Wow."

"Ethiopian coffee."

"Fabulous. How?"

"Anunaki sent out a drone. Secret mission of sorts."

"Why didn't you tell me?"

"It's a surprise, meu amor."

"Thank you, sweetheart."

"Now, let's get to work."

Three days later the Eden Manifesto digitally hangs on the external Bubble wall; one at every access point. It reads as follows:

Welcome To Eden
Place of health, healing and happiness.
Venue of love, kindness and compassion.
Home of peace, respect, freedom and joy.
Leave your ideologies and clothes outside.
You enter naked and with no possessions.
First cleansing then body measurements.
Wait by the 3D printer for your robe.
Taxis take you to induction centre.
Walk quietly. Leave no footprints.

I shrug and smile.

It's simple. It's enough.

* * *

"We need to import those experts."

"I know. I know."

Eva is haranguing me. Why am I procrastinating? Am I apprehensive about sharing power? Perhaps I am worried about others' influence on our beautiful world. Or is it the scars from the current disdainful political systems on Earth? There has to be a new system based on love, truth and respect.

Casting my mind to the vision of leadership.

Eva and I holding hands, standing at the top of a huge pyramid. Just below us the Council of Light, encircling the apex of the pyramid, clasping each other's wrists, singing, chanting, praying, meditating. Below them a band of learned individuals, experts in various fields, proffering knowledge, debating, implementing.

Layers and layers of beings descending all the way down to the base of the pyramid.

"We need to bring in the Council of Light. The new world requires spiritual then intellectual leadership. The learned experts must report to the Council. After that we can have layers of national and local governance."

She nods fervidly.

"Let's make it happen."

"Before I contact them, can we access your gift of Knowledge?"

"Sure. You want to do it now?"

"If you don't mind."

She lays on the sofa and closes her eyes.

I command the wall lume to record the conversation.

Hmm ... An unresolved query.

"What happened at the Christ the Redeemer statue?"

Her voice becomes calm and surreal.

"It was time."

"Yes ..."

"The Golden Age."

"Uh huh ..."

"Return of the Christ energy."

"And that dazzling orb that entered you?"

"A piece of Christ consciousness."

"Is this connected to your dream about the birds?"

"The dream I had that same night?"

"Yes. A flock of 144,000 Jenday Conures chirping in the heavens."

She giggles quietly.

"12 x 12,000 = 144,000."

"Meaning?"

"Golden Age ... it's time ..."

"Wait a minute. Are there now 144,000 pieces of Christ consciousness on Earth?"

"Yes."

"Inside selected human souls?"

"Yes. The merging of consciousness."

"Are those the experts who should guide our world?"

"Yes!"

"How do we find them?"

"You know the answer."

"Follow the energy?"

"Indeed."

"Are those beings advanced enough for Eden?"

"You are doing a threat analysis?"

I blush slightly.

"Adam, you worry too much. What is the gateway to higher consciousness and power?"

"Spiritual maturity."

"The 144,000 were carefully chosen."

"Are they all the same?"

"Different personalities, traits and dispositions. All have the Christ consciousness."

"Richness in diversity."

"Those beings need to be spread throughout Eden and eventually Earth."

"The Bubble is not large enough."

"Expand Eden."

"Alright."

"Remember the words of Ra?"

"'You need revolution not evolution.'"

"Exactly."

Her eyes flutter open.

"Did you record everything?"

"Of course, sweetheart."

I play the session back.

There is a fire growing in her eyes. Never seen her like this before.

Pensive nod.

"Do you mind if we separate for a while?"

"What?"

"You need to summon and brief the Council of Light."

"Will do."

"I need to locate some of the 144,000."

"Can't we go together?"

Agitated stare.

"The clock is ticking. The world is in turmoil. New leadership and systems are required."

Holding my head in my hands.

"I don't want to be a lone ranger anymore."

"You are my kindred spirit. We will be together forever."

"How long will you be gone?"

She brushes her hand against my cheek.

"Give me the Loophole so I can leap home."

I pluck the silver circle and give it to her.

"We are love rangers now, not lone rangers."

A smile overcomes my face.

She pulls me into a tight embrace.

"I will leave in the morning."

A knife pricks my heart.

We talk late into the night. Cuddle closely. Shed a few tears.

Needless to say, I get very little sleep.

In the morning she is awake early. I hear her busy in the washroom for long time.

When she finally emerges I am stunned.

"Eva, what on earth happened?"

"I permanently removed all my hair."

"Why? Couldn't you consult me first?"

"Time to walk our talk. We need to lead by example."

"What's the hair to do with anything?"

"No more gender stereotypes. No more judging a woman by her hair and make-up. Eden needs to be a world where every person can 'Be real. Be free.'"

"Is that your new slogan?"

"Yes. I want it added to the bottom of the Manifesto."

"Seriously?"

"Yes."

"Okay."

"Apart from eyebrows and eyelashes, body hair serves no purpose. Eden is temperature-regulated. Every day is a warm summer's day. Anyway, if I am really cold I can raise my hood."

"You decided to wear a robe now?"

"Yes. You were right."

"I was?"

She nods adamantly.

"You said 'I could wear the same thing every day, especially if those nanofibres can change colour and pattern.'"

"I remember."

"The 3D printer builds a perfect customised robe. I can adjust colour and pattern according to my mood. It is light, protective, waterproof, self-cleaning, temperature-regulated, and the liquid crystallinity results in a wearable lume. It is the obvious practical choice."

"Indeed."

"Plus I will no longer be judged by my appearance."

She looks at me coyly.

"You still love me for who I am?"

I stride into the washroom, remove my clothing, stand in front of the mirror, and command complete hair removal *sans* eyebrows and eyelashes. The entire process takes twenty minutes.

Eva is standing in the doorway watching me.

I gaze at my new bald head and body then turn toward her.

"Here's your answer."

She rushes over and kisses me passionately.

"I love you with all my heart and soul and mind."

"I love you to Arcturus and back."

"Will you amend the Manifesto?"

"I will."

"And change the settings so that anyone who enters Eden is cleansed *and* epilated, apart from eyebrows and eyelashes."

"Wow. It's a whole new world."

"Be real. Be free."

"Where will you start?"

"Brazil. I know my way around."

"Come home soon."

"I will, meu amor."

Intense hug. Deep kiss.

Casts the Loophole.

She is gone.

* * *

Her absence leaves me reeling.

My shift from loner to lover was unmitigated and incontrovertible. I had no idea the depth and speed of my conversion. It is irrevocable. There is no way back.

I am left with a terrible ache in my heart and soul.

Is it harder because she is a soul mate and kindred spirit?

My only choice is to proceed with the mission.

Eva and I are essentially visionaries and directors.

We can no longer operate alone. I need to summon the Council of Light while she is away gathering members of the 144,000.

I quickly update the Manifesto. It now reads as follows:

Welcome To Eden
Place of health, healing and happiness.
Venue of love, kindness and compassion.
Home of peace, respect, freedom and joy.
Leave your ideologies and clothes outside.
You enter naked and with no possessions.
Cleansing, epilation, body measurement.
Wait by the 3D printer for your robe.
Taxis take you to induction centre.
Walk quietly. Leave no footprints.
Be real. Be free.

I activate the Adi Shakti and contact the twelve members of the Council of Light, including the successor to Q'ero Shaman Chuya (who mysteriously disappeared after the battle of Machu Picchu). Only one member is resistant to the entrance requirements. Unfortunately, it is not a negotiation. Eleven will have to do for now.

A few days later I travel to the NE1 access point to welcome my beloved friends and light-workers. It is a joyous and heartfelt reunion. Familiar greetings and jests abound.

"We were thinking you'd forgotten us, Adam."

"Aisatsu! Ready for a challenge!"

"Sanibonani!"

"Epilation be upon you!"

"Um waynuma?"

"Rimaykullayki!"

Once the group is assembled at the Hall of Learning in the first city, I explain the functions of the brilliant Capuchin robes. An hour disappears while each member profiles their garment to suit their particular penchants and predilections.

I have to acknowledge that Eva's ideas are working. Everyone is wearing the same, albeit customised, clothing and we all have a fairly similar appearance. The focus will now be on our spirits, hearts and minds. Zero extraneous distractions.

The Council of Light are a lively bunch. I explain my vision of a new world. First perfecting Eden then extending it across the planet. Eden is essentially a microcosm of future Earth. We need to make the mistakes here, follow the learning curve, improve, refine, and finally reveal something extraordinary and delightful to everyone.

A spirited discussion ensues.

Sikh Nanak: "What is our purpose?"

Zen Master Koichi: "Simplicity and spontaneity."

African Shaman Iboga: "Spiritual nurturing."

Q'ero Shaman Akllasumaq: "Teaching the multi-dimensions."

African Shaman Iboga: "Wielding the higher energies."

Aboriginal Elder Mandu: "Connecting to the ancestors."

Klamath Elder Láshaltko: "Love, kindness and compassion."

Hopi Mystic Qaletaqa: "Embracing the Source."

Imam Abu Talib: "Integrity, impeccability, maturity."

Aboriginal Elder Mandu: "Healing and dreaming."

Hopi Mystic Qaletaqa: "Transcendence."

I glance across the oval table at the other members.

Pensive, thoughtful, contemplative.

Raising my hand.

"Yes. All of the above."

It suddenly becomes still.

Shimmering surreal energy.

Why is the mystical author gazing out the window?

I stand up and survey the desolate landscape.

There is someone down there. And he is not bald.

How can this be?

I notice the author smiling and waving.

Long flowing white robe ... pure white hair cascading over his shoulders ... white eyebrows, white moustache ... white eyelashes ... almond-shaped piercing blue eyes that reach across the distance and leap into my soul.

Arms outstretched.

Shock of brilliant light.

Build the temples, Adam.

The words burrow into my mind.

Build the temples, Adam.

An extraordinary calmness flows over me. My shoulders relax and my breathing deepens. Clarity ripples through my consciousness.

I lean my palms on the table, slowly gaze at each member.

"We are the spiritual leaders of planet Earth. It's time to put aside our ritualistic differences and focus on true spirituality. Each one of us has been initiated into the Mystery, surfed the multi-dimensions, entered the Light. This is what we need to bring to the people of Earth. We must build temples at every city of Eden."

Zen Master Koichi: "I am sensing that too."

Aboriginal Elder Mandu: "One Way. Truth, Love, Light."

Klamath Elder Láshaltko: "Build the temples, train apprentices. We cannot be everywhere."

African Shaman Iboga: "Our Tribe will become overseers. We have a planet to nurture."

Q'ero Shaman Akllasumaq: "Wise words, my friend."

I turn my head toward Iboga. "What did you say? Tribe?"

She beams a radiant smile.

African Shaman Iboga: "We are one Tribe. Spiritual warriors. Light-workers."

Q'ero Shaman Akllasumaq: "One Tribe. Mystical teachers."

Imam Abu Talib: "One Tribe. Spiritual leaders."

It all goes quiet. The air seems to be vibrating around us. We sense the presence of the beings of light, of the angels, of the multi-dimensional entities. It's a blessing. A tacit endorsement of our words and intentions. We are on the right path.

After a few minutes the author speaks: "Let's draw up plans. The temples can take inspiration from churches, cathedrals, mosques, synagogues, gurdwaras, mandirs, monasteries, stupas, pagodas, and other shrines and sacred places."

I take a deep breath.

"There will be only three temples. They will be duplicated at each city, and eventually throughout the planet. We will locate them in the outer limits of the city spirals, where it is quietest and surrounded by lush nature."

African Shaman Iboga: "Why three temples?"

"Healing. Teaching. Transcendence."

I gesture to the large wall lume; index finger moving, digital writing appears.

"The first temple will be primarily for spiritual and emotional healing; clearing negative and dark energy; resolving past life issues; repairing energy wounds; restoring fragmented consciousness; and so forth."

Q'ero Shaman Akllasumaq: "Will this temple have a designation?"

"Mystical Divine Magical Awakening Temple."

Imam Abu Talib: "That's a mouthful."

Zen Master Koichi: "It can be condensed into an acronym."

Nonchalant shrug.

"Whatever. That's the name."

Klamath Elder Láshaltko: "And the second temple?"

My face lights up.

"You're going to love this one."

African Shaman Iboga: "Share with us."

"Ecstatic Tantra."

Q'ero Shaman Akllasumaq: "Tantra? That's a specialised field."

Aboriginal Elder Mandu: "To cultivate loving relationships."

"Intimacy, integration, awakening."

Imam Abu Talib: "Where is our twelfth member?"

"Tantrika Amrita?"

He nods inquisitively.

"She refused to acquiesce to the entry requirements."

Sikh Nanak: "Remove her long luscious hair?"

I fold my arms and grin.

"Not at all. She loves being nude all over. In fact, that's the problem. She doesn't want to wear anything."

Imam Abu Talib: "Not even a robe?"

Shaking my head.

"Maybe we can convince her to wear a robe when she leaves the temple."

Zen Master Koichi: "She'll adore this nanofibre when she sees it."

"I hope so."

Buddhist Monk Sangye: "What of the third temple?"

"Transcendence."

Questioning stare.

"Travelling into the Light."

Christian Mystic Francis: "Meeting the Source."

"Embracing the multi-dimensions along the way."

Aboriginal Elder Mandu: "Does this temple have a name?"

"Light Source Dimension Temple."

Sikh Nanak: "I suppose it makes sense."

Zen Master Koichi: "Begging for another acronym."

Hopi Mystic Qaletaqa: "Brilliant. That's where I'll be working."

I take a deep breath.

"We need to design these temples with spiritual motifs, mystical decor and inspiring ambience. The psychophysiological environment is crucial when commencing healing and transcendent journeys. Let's throw ideas into the lume."

I summon Anunaki.

"This is Eden's chief AI machine. It will coordinate our efforts. Ask it anything."

The silver-blue humanoid bows before the Council of Light.

Ready to serve.

Diverse suggestions are articulated. An array of concepts and illustrations are gestured into the wall lume. In turn, Anunaki tenders vivid and elaborate holographic designs.

An incoming call interrupts the work. It's the Tantrika.

Tantrika Amrita: "Hey, you're not starting without me?"

Retorts and jests ripple across the table.

I smile sweetly.

"Ignore them. They're overexcited."

Tantrika Amrita: "About what?"

Zen Master Koichi approaches the wall lume. "Peruse this gorgeous robe. Light, self-cleaning, protective, waterproof, temperature-regulated."

Tantrika Amrita: "Yes, and …?"

He transitions the robe gradually from Zen-like black to psychedelic jungle colours to sky blue with sponge-painted honeycomb and paprika.

Tantrika Amrita: "Wow."

I raise my palms and shrug.

"Your Capuchin robe will be customised to your body measurements."

Tantrika Amrita: "Tempting."

"We are busy designing the Ecstatic Tantra Temple."

Tantrika Amrita: "Not without me! Can I at least be naked in the temple?"

"Absolutely."

A moment of silence.

Tantrika Amrita: "On my way. Hold those designs."

"Okay. See you soon."

Twelve members of the Council of Light. Three glorious temples.

Spiritual leadership is approaching this planet.

Our Tribe is coming together.

Eden is manifesting.

* * *

A month has passed.

The first temples have been built and they look spectacular. Huge, ornate, life-affirming, heartening, inspiring.

Ecstatic Tantra Temple is embellished with rich warm intense colours, scarlet-golden furnishings, cosy thick-pile rugs, scatter cushions, fabric hearts, evocative digital art and dramatic yantras.

Mystical Divine Magical Awakening Temple is an immersion into nature. Sky blues, pine greens, earth tones, abundant indoor plants. Comfortable airy spaces. Immense statues of prominent religious and mystical figures. Wall lumes displaying joyful loving scenes. Soothing sofas, nurturing rooms, snug alcoves, soft ochre blankets. Imbued with welcoming, safe, supportive energy.

Light Source Dimension Temple is expansive, marblesque, Zen-like, decorated in radiant white with intermittent streaks of mauve. It is spacious, serene and minimalist, encouraging the journey beyond earthly reality. Here you leave everything behind and leap into the multi-dimensions. Here you embrace the Light. Here you meet God.

I am very pleased and proud of our progress.

Anunaki and the AI machines are now rapidly constructing more cities, along with the concomitant temples. It won't be long until Eden is complete.

The Council is jubilant and celebratory. There are more discussions around the oval table. Induction programmes; safety measures; training of mentors, healers and carers; courses for teachers and apprentices; operating principles and guidelines; and the eventual role of the Council.

My heart is indifferent to dialogue and debate. I am staring out the window, wondering about Eva. Where is she? What has happened to her?

Activate the lume and request connection. No answer.

Should I be concerned?

An hour later the wall lume flashes red. Activity at the perimeter. Scanning the NE1 access point. It's Eva! My heart starts racing. She is bringing people into Eden. Initiating cleansing, epilation and robe measurement. Who are they?

I send a message via the Bubble, explaining that we are in the Hall of Learning. She quickly acknowledges, confirming they will join us shortly.

The Council has quit their discourse. Watching the monitor intently.

Sikh Nanak: "Adam, what's happening?"

I feel a bit apprehensive.

"Not really sure. I think these are members of the 144,000."

Zen Master Koichi: "The 144,000?"

"It's a long story. Human souls imbued with Christ consciousness. Gifted experts. The next level of the pyramid."

African Shaman Iboga: "What pyramid?"

"The Council of Light are the spiritual leaders of the new world. All of you sit at the top of the pyramid. As you can imagine, you will gradually learn to operate at the highest level, with the broadest perspective."

Q'ero Shaman Akllasumaq: "More big picture. Less hands-on."

"Exactly. The level below you are gifted experts, specialists in various fields. Although they are definitely hands-on, eventually they too must develop a global perspective."

Klamath Elder Láshaltko: "And the next level?"

"National and local governance. Hopefully a different form of politics."

Imam Abu Talib: "Legislative and pragmatic leadership."

"Yep. No idea how that will unfold."

Hopi Mystic Qaletaqa: "In a world not influenced by money and power, the right people will choose to serve and lead."

"I hope that's true."

Aboriginal Elder Mandu: "The Council of Light will be exemplars of Truth, Love and Light to the people of this planet. Eden will offer ideal living conditions and optimal environments. The rest will follow naturally."

Convivial smile. Gaze at them earnestly.

"Sagacious leaders of the new world."

I bow reverently.

The Council stands and bows in return.

Here comes Eva with a cluster of newcomers.

"Hey, sweetheart!"

"Hey, meu amor!"

We rush into a close embrace.

Soft whisper: "Missed you. Glad you're home."

Ah. Those radiant blue eyes, gorgeous smile!

She steps back, waves her palm.

"Adam, Council, please welcome the Gifted."

Surveying the freshly epilated enrobed men and women. Strangers in a strange world. They're probably more anxious than us.

"Twelve so far, hopefully more to arrive soon."

After ebullient greetings and brief conversation, Eva introduces her "Tribe". I have to smile. Is that what we are now? Two Tribes?

The titles say it all: Terraformer – Landscaper – Botanist – Zoologist – Geneticist – Medical Doctor – Scientist – Philosopher – Master of Education – Senator – Engineer – Entertainment Executive.

I have a curious feeling we have to surrender and trust. No other way forward.

The Council and the Gifted can mingle and acclimatise for a while.

As for me, I grab Eva and whisk her away for some alone time.

Delicious reacquainting is in order.

* * *

Eden is a flurry of activity.

Everyone is settling into their roles, aware that our world is a template for future Earth. A huge responsibility rests on our shoulders. We need to consolidate all designs, principles and procedures, remove any flaws, then tweak and perfect. Nothing less than awe-inspiring will do.

As the construction of Eden nears completion, the Engineer approaches me about inter-city transport. I hadn't really thought about it. The Bubble, of course, covers an area of 1,000 square kilometres. There will be 100 cities. The self-driving taxis only operate within each city.

He proposes a high-speed rail network elevated above the cities, following the perimeter of the Bubble and running lengthwise north and south in a grid formation. Rail stations would be located at every city centre.

My mind flashes to my brief stay at Area 51. The discovery of an underground pod-transport system called the Heisenberg Train. Something to do with collapsing wave-functions and instantaneous travel. Way beyond my knowledge-base.

I summon Anunaki. The Engineer and the machine converse for a long while. Eventually Anunaki produces a complex hologram. A silent instantaneous above-ground travel network. Designed to blended seamlessly and elegantly with our cities and natural environments. It will be called the Elon.

It's an impressive design. Once the parameters are clearly defined, I surrender the project to the Engineer. I surmise this is leadership. Holding the vision, establishing rigid parameters, tapping the experts, allocating resources, then setting people free to do the work. Always that old lesson: Surrender and trust.

Eva has been engaging frenetically with the Terraformer, Landscaper and Botanist. As construction of our magnificent cities nears completion, the contrast with the bleak terrain has become starkly pronounced. Many people have stepped in to assist: Tantrika Amrita, Zen Master Koichi, African Shaman Iboga, Q'ero Shaman Akllasumaq, Buddhist Monk Sangye, the Senator and the Entertainment Executive.

I am looking forward to the result of their blended perspectives and expertise.

Now it's time to consider a romantic way to propose to Eva.

I wonder if we will use engagement rings in Eden. Will there be novel rituals and protocols in a world without money and power? Eva seems to be fostering a culture of loving-kindness and non-judgement. Her principal tenet is 'Be real. Be free.' She has already banned make-up. A glittering diamond on her finger would probably be regarded as unnecessary glamour.

Perhaps Tantrika Amrita has a few ideas. I activate the lume and schedule a clandestine meeting at her temple. She is free later in the morning.

The Tantrika does not consume caffeine or sugar, so I quietly enjoy my cappuccino in the courtyard of our lovely home. The sky is glimmering brightly through the translucent sheen of the Bubble. Another perfect day in Eden.

When we meet up, she is her usual forthright self. She gives me an affectionate hug.

"Good to feel you. Still on the caffeine?"

I blush slightly.

"Yeah."

She shakes her head.

"If you want to experience Tantric ecstasy, you need to abstain from all dietary stimulants."

"All of them?"

"Your body is a finely tuned temple with the capacity for phenomenal pleasure and physiological bliss. Your body contains the foundation for emotional and spiritual ecstasy."

"Sounds juicy."

She shrugs.

"You'll be ready one day. What can I do for you?"

"I want to propose to Eva."

Genial laughter fills the air.

"Well done!"

"Any advice?"

"Keep it simple. No jewellery or possession indicators. Use a grand gesture."

"We don't even have flowers to pick yet."

Her brow furrows intently.

"You do know that plants have consciousness? Flowers belong in nature."

"Ah. I'll keep that in mind."

"The food replicators scientifically create delicious nutritious food. There is absolutely no need to harm animals and plants."

I nod my head solemnly.

"Eva has a resolute philosophy: 'Be real. Be free.'"

"That should apply to all beings, not just humans."

Wow. I hadn't even considered that. Perhaps I should be spending more time with the Tantrika.

Tilt my head and frown.

"What about domestic pets?"

She takes a deep breath.

"Animals should be free. Why do we enslave them? Circuses and zoos are abhorrent and have no place in Eden. Do you know why people have pets?"

"Tell me."

"They live in atomised societies instead of tribal societies. Their world feels uncaring, detached and segregated. Money, power, technology and frivolous media are the primary focus. People have suppressed their deepest need."

"Which need?"

"Heart connection."

"You mean love?"

"Intimacy. Into-me-I-see. Into-you-I-see."

"Sweet words."

"Eden must be a tribal society. We need to infuse this world with unconditional love, kindness, acceptance, non-judgement and deep intimacy."

"And freedom."

She stares into my eyes.

"Do you know what my teacher taught me?"

"I'm listening."

"The journey of Tantra is the wildest exposure of one's own heart and the most loving acceptance of another's heart."

A warm tear wells in my eye.

"The words of Śakra."

"Indeed."

"He was your teacher?"

"Uh huh."

She pulls me into a close embrace.

"Every being is precious. Every being is beloved."

She is right. Emotional and spiritual intimacy are essential. We need a world where people are seen, heard and deeply connected. We need to teach people to live freely and authentically, leading with their hearts and souls.

A brief movement catches my attention.

In the distance ... long white hair ... piercing blue eyes.

Burst of brilliant energy.

Adam.

Amrita is still clasping my shoulders.

Adam.

An extraordinary peace courses through me.

One Tribe.

I nod sagaciously.

One Love.

I nod tearfully.

One Planet.

I nod joyfully.

A thought sparks in my mind.

Eden is almost complete. Time to smooth the edges.

I bow graciously to Amrita.

"Sublime wisdom."

Returns the bow.

"Love is All."

* * *

I am reluctant to start a tradition. However, my proposal was memorable. I lit up the entire inner wall of the Bubble with an enormous sentence: 'Eva, will you marry me?'

Needless to say, the answer was 'Yes, Adam!'

The mood in Eden is ebullient. We are completing the finishing touches. Everyone is feeling satisfied and celebratory. It is just a matter of weeks.

I am strolling through the new landscape. At last we are immersed in nature. The white buildings and community-trees are coolly counterpointed with the verdant green environment. Architecturally and artistically exquisite.

Breathing the pure fresh air of Eden. Gazing at the abundant trees and plants, the copious butterflies and birds, the sea of luminous flowers. How utterly delightful. I have missed all this. Nature truly recharges the body and revitalises the soul.

Eva, Amrita, Iboga and the Landscaper are busy planning our wedding. It is only a few days away. Eva has insisted that we stay 'on message' and lead by example, so we'll be wearing our robes. However, we have quietly agreed to restyle them into glimmering white for the occasion.

When the day arrives I am surprisingly nervous. I have known Eva for a relatively short time. So much has happened. Barely a moment to pause and absorb everything. I console myself with the knowledge that she is my soul mate and kindred spirit. I love her immensely.

Tantrika Amrita is marrying us. Twenty-three attendees are seated on ochre blankets on the lush hilltop next to the Ecstatic Tantra Temple. The view is spectacular, an indirect acknowledgement of our vision and hard work. Amrita delivers a beautiful message about communication, acceptance and loving-kindness. She nods to the Landscaper who is seated just behind us. I glance back, intrigued.

The Landscaper pushes her fingers into the ground. She utters a few strange words. Within moments a climbing rose appears in the grass beside us. It quickly twists along the large heart-shaped trellis under which we are standing. I watch in awe as it blooms with profuse multi-coloured flowers. Spectacular, gorgeous, enchanting.

I bow courteously. So that's the Gift! Knowledge and power in a specialised field. It explains how Eden suddenly blossomed into a glorious garden of huge trees and bountiful vegetation.

A sweet scent wafts through the air. Amrita asks us to face each other and clasp our right hands. She holds a purple ribbon above her head, speaks a sacred incantation, then gently wraps it around our wrists and fingers. Our left hands remain unencumbered.

A brief explanation is given:

"Handfasting is a formal ritual and promise used in a wedding ceremony. The term originates from the Old Norse *handfesta* meaning 'to strike a bargain by joining hands'. Marriage vows may be for 'a year', 'a lifetime' or 'for all eternity'. Wrapping the marrying couple's right hands symbolises commitment and intimacy. The left hands remain unclasped and unfettered which symbolises independence and freedom."

Amrita invites us to declare our vows.

I gaze lovingly into Eva's radiant blue eyes.

"Today I take you to be my wife. I promise to love you unconditionally, cherish you, listen to you, laugh with you, cry with you, adore you, and lavish affection and cuddles upon you. I vow to walk with you in Truth, Love and Light. I will always be open and honest with you. I pledge the wildest exposure of my heart and the most loving acceptance of your heart."

"Today I take you to be my husband. I promise to love you unconditionally, cherish you, respect you, listen to you, support you, and lavish delicious yumminess upon you. Together we will explore the realms of Ecstatic Tantra. I vow to walk with you in Surrender and Trust. I pledge to be caring and truthful, to love you just as you are, and to grow old by your side as your best friend and kindred spirit."

"For all eternity."

"For all eternity."

Amrita seals the ceremony: "And so it is."

The guests melodiously intone: "And so it is."

We embrace and kiss passionately.

Ebullient applause. Prolific hugs, handshakes and kisses.

Iboga hands out large picnic baskets and we huddle on the blankets.

Music, mirth and merriment continue until midnight.

11 November. The best day of my interesting life.

And tomorrow ... the dawn of a new phase.

We strategise the expansion of Eden.

A gift for planet Earth.

* * *

And right on schedule, as if the gods have been monitoring our progress, the wall lume in our bedroom lights up early in the morning. Ra and Baset are requesting access at NE1.

The gods will not be a permanent feature of our new world, so I forego the standard entrance requirements. Anyway, Ra is already bald and enrobed, and Baset is in the form of a cat. She will be the first animal to enter Eden.

I despatch a taxi to bring them to the Hall of Learning, hop into the waterless shower, then hurriedly devour a chocolate croissant and tepid cappuccino. I call Eva along the way. She is busy with the Landscaper and will join us later.

A smiles brushes my face. My wife is headstrong and determined. Admirable qualities when it comes to leadership. Brilliant traits for fulfilling a mission. However, she doesn't forget a slight. I don't think she has completely forgiven Tefnut. And she has not established a close connection with Ra. No wonder they were not invited to our wedding. Hope they will not be upset.

The sun-god greets me with a big hug. It still surprises me. Always knew him as brusque and blunt; now he is more like a relaxed grizzly bear. Still, I tread carefully around him.

"Hey, Ra ... Baset ..."

Those intense green eyes stare up at me. Does that cat ever chill out? Perhaps she only respects brazen strength. Hmm ... gives me an idea.

Ra slides his arm across my shoulders.

You going to give us a tour?

I nod.

"Eden is almost complete. The Council and the Gifted have been working strategically and diligently. Together we have created something magnificent."

The Gifted?

Ah. He doesn't know. Excellent.

"Yep. Experts in various fields. Part of the plan to redesign and upgrade Earth."

He glances at Baset. No doubt signalling her to investigate. She scurries off.

Two hours later we have covered the entire grid.

The sun-god is admiring the Japanese Cherry Blossoms that cocoon the Light Source Dimension Temple. He is delicately caressing the pink and white flowers.

This cherry blossom is known as 'sakura'. It is native to the Himalayas.

I survey the lush terrain. The word sounds like Śakra. Evokes poignant memories of our time in the Himalayas. Blinking away the tears.

Ra smiles kindly.

I miss him too. If it's any consolation, this tour has been relayed to the Star Child. He is very proud of what you have achieved. Sends his love to both of you. The Guardian of the Earth is also very pleased.

Pensive nod.

So ... what's next?

Timing. Here comes Baset.

Deep breath. Stand tall, make direct eye contact.

"Revolution. Expansion of Eden."

You will meet resistance from the outside.

"That's why you are going to run interference for me."

I gaze down at Baset.

"The gods are going to fulfil their promise. Meet with world leaders. Campaign to the public. Assuage fears. Advertise the benefits."

What's your timetable?

"1ˢᵗ January. Expansion state by state through North America and Canada. Perhaps you can spin it as a Christmas gift."

Smiling to myself. The dissemination of Christ consciousness.

Ra nods solemnly.

Alright. It's your world. You and Eva are leaders.

Baset purrs acquiescently.

Ha! I did it. Finally stepped into my power. It's not about ego. It's about my role and purpose. It's about communicating and commanding respect.

"You can tell the world we are waiting for them. It's time to join the Tribe. You need to publicise the Eden Manifesto."

Welcome To Eden
Place of health, healing and happiness.
Venue of love, kindness and compassion.
Home of peace, respect, freedom and joy.
Leave your ideologies and clothes outside.
You enter naked and with no possessions.
Cleansing, epilation, body measurement.
Wait by the 3D printer for your robe.
Taxis take you to induction centre.
Walk quietly. Leave no footprints.
Be real. Be free.

Right on cue, Eva arrives and nods courteously.

"Have I missed anything?"

"No, sweetheart. Ra and Baset have accepted their assignment."

"Prepare the external world?"

"Yep."

She turns toward them.

"You understand the schedule?"

The energy field speaks far louder than words.

Eva reaches across and holds my hand.

Ra bows deferentially. Baset sits quietly at his feet.

Suddenly she leaps into Eva's arms. Purring and bunting into her neck.

Something shifts. Heart feels warm. Ice melting.

I step forward and embrace the sun-god.

"Thank you for everything."

Luminous smile.

All will be well.

I laugh exultantly. If you wait long enough, everything works out. As long as you hold your vision, set clear intentions, acquire knowledge, take appropriate action and keep learning. In the end, all will be well.

Eva hails a taxi and we say our goodbyes.

We need to convene a tribal meeting.

The metaphysical Tribe of Eden.

Twinkling of an Eye.

* * *

We wake up to find a message emblazoned on the inner wall of the Bubble: 'Koichi, will you marry me?'

Hmm. Appears I have started a tradition.

I roll toward Eva and cuddle in her bosom.

"Who sent that?"

She ruffles my hair.

"You don't know?"

I shrug.

"Koichi was holding Amrita's hand at the wedding."

"Really?"

"Men! You seldom notice the clues."

"Are they in love?"

"For the longest time."

"Wow. Imagine the synthesis. Zen Master and Tantrika."

"Yeah. I am imagining ..."

I kiss my wife's breasts affectionately. Then stray my lips onto her soft tummy.

"Mmm ... while you're down there ..."

Glance at her playfully.

"Is that a request?"

She directs my head toward her yoni.

I respond willingly.

Nuzzling the sacred space.

"Love your delicious scent."

Gentle luscious licks. Soft teasing flicks.

Wrapping my tongue around her engorged clio.

She writhes and moans. Caresses my hair.

"Oh, that's good, meu amor ... up a little ... oh my ... move two fingers inside me ... yes ... oh yes ... oh ... oh ... keep doing that ... oh ... oh ... don't stop ..."

Her pleasurable cries fill the air.

After she has finished trembling, she pulls me toward her face. We kiss passionately. She stares at me with the deepest love.

"Fill me with your lingam. Make love with me."

Nature's rhythm blends with our souls.

Our hearts are intertwining.

Ambience becomes serene.

"I love you, Eva."

"I love you too."

Surrendering …

Overwhelming …

Exquisite ecstasy …

We lay for a long while, cuddling in each other's arms.

Her brow furrows.

"The future is almost upon us."

"I feel apprehensive and excited."

"Will the world like us? Will they accept the rules and parameters?"

"We are offering so much. Perfect health. All survival needs met. Clean air. Nutritious food. Gorgeous environment. Freedom to live and work as they choose. And the cost?"

"Be respectful. Be kind. Be real. Be free."

"That's hardly a cost. Every society has its norms."

She holds me tight.

"Tell me it's going to be alright."

"Everything will be perfect."

"Are you sure?"

"Love will conquer all."

I stare at the ceiling, contemplating the impending changes.

"Hey, should we do another session?"

"Access my gift of Knowledge?"

"Yes. Might be soothing."

"Okay. If I jump in the shower, will you sort breakfast?"

"Deal. See you in five."

I love the food replicator. The healthiest and tastiest meals from a simple voice command or press of a button. The recent upgrades have already been rolled out. The Medical Doctor, Scientist and Engineer have devised a brilliant system. Every washroom has been retrofitted with an invisible medical scanner which constantly updates the home 3D printer and food replicator with body measurements and health data. Clothing is automatically customised and food nutritionally optimised for each individual. All information is stored on the lume system and at Medical Services. Best of all, the food replicator now offers a vast menu, capable of satisfying the most diverse palates.

Returning with a loaded tray. Eva's favourite breakfast smoothies, croissants, toasted bread rolls, mandatory pingado and cappuccino. Yummylicious.

Half an hour later, she lays her head on the pillow.

"Ready when you are."

Closes her eyes.

Hmm ... What to ask?

"The 144,000. We only have a few here in Eden. Should we be contacting the rest?"

"You are the leaders of this world. You are creating this reality."

"Meaning?"

"As always, choices."

"They are a vital part of new Earth. We need to induct them before the expansion of Eden."

"You have a question?"

"Is there a way to contact the Gifted?"

"Eva can create an energy beacon to draw them."

"How?"

"Intention. Christ consciousness."

"Aha."

Rubbing my chin.

"Where does this information originate?"

"Akasha."

"Ak-what-now?"

"The Fifth Element."

"Excuse me?"

"Quintessence."

"Please explain."

I hear the deep sigh.

"Reality comprises four elements."

"Yes?"

"Earth, water, fire, air."

"Okay."

"And aether."

"What's aether?"

"The mysterious Fifth Element, the quintessence of the universe."

"The manifested universe?"

"Yes."

"That's different to the Source?"

"The Source is the unmanifested underlying Is-ness, the ocean of possibility."

"Aha."

She sighs again.

"What did Sikh Nanak teach you about Shakti?"

"'There exists nothing but God and his Shakti. God is the unmanifested observer and she is the embodiment of his dreams. She creates all the universes with her endless love. She in fact *is* the creation. All of creation is merely a beautiful cloak to wrap God in and make him visible.'"

"Aether is that beautiful cloak. Akasha is the Sanskrit word for aether."

"I understand."

"From that quintessence, air, fire, water and earth descend."

"Those four elements are readily visible."

"All living beings are immersed in the Fifth Element. It is visible to those who see."

"Elucidate."

"The twinkling of an Eye."

"That phrase popped into my head yesterday."

"Every thought, word and deed is recorded in the Akasha. To be precise, all creation and manifestation *is* the Akasha."

"The Out-Breath of God."

"The Fifth Element is spirit."

"We are not only immersed in the Fifth Element. We are the Fifth Element."

"Yes!"

"We use our spiritual eyes to see the Fifth Element."

"Twinkling of the Eye to view the Akasha."

Hmm ... I wonder ...

"Is each point of consciousness composed of five aspects?"

"Seven aspects."

A magnificent thought enters my mind.

"We are the layers of Existence."

"I'm listening."

"Base or root chakra is the earth; sacral chakra is the water; solar plexus chakra is the fire; heart chakra is the air; throat chakra is the primordial sound Aum; third-eye chakra is the Akashic Eye; crown chakra is the Source."

Eva is beaming a huge smile.

"You have graduated!"

It's my turn to smile.

Wow. For the first time I truly get it.

"Every journey follows the same path: Love, Awareness, Kundalini rising, Awakening, Enlightenment, Being Home."

My consciousness is rapidly expanding.

Observing the cosmic network. Vibrating filaments of Light. All connected. Here I am. Journey this way or that way. Multitudinous intersecting paths. Manifestation or dispensation. Creation or dissolution. Thought or No-Thought. Always the choices. Choices, choices, choices.

Head feels like it's going to explode.

"I know too much! I see too much!"

Calming voice.

"Surrender, Adam. Surrender and trust."

Hilarious tears. Overwhelming vibration.

Boom! The Light. Immersion. All That Is.

Freedom. Bliss. Oneness.

"I Am! I Am!"

"I Am."

"I Am."

* * *

"Hey, sleepyhead."

"What happened? How long have I been out?"

"You dozed off for an hour."

"I feel different."

"You are."

"I Am."

"Played back the recording. Wow."

Running my fingers through my hair.

"Did you create the energy beacon yet?"

"Uh huh. We don't falter on my shift."

"We'll soon be inundated by the 144,000."

"That's the plan, my darling."

I have to smile. Adore this woman.

"Oh yeah. Minor modification to Eden's programming. Capuchin robes will be the only nanofibre clothing. This will encourage their use in the new world. All other clothing will be regular mundane material."

"Then let's make sandals and ankle boots the only nanofibre footwear."

Exuberant nod.

"Agreed."

"We need to schedule a tribal meeting for later this afternoon."

"Already done."

Clamber off the bed and head to the washroom.

"Long overdue for a shower."

She crinkles her nose.

"That's for sure."

"Hey!"

"Just teasing, meu amor."

I have slowly adapted to the waterless shower. No billowing steam or cascading wetness. Instead, luscious radiance that cleanses and caresses the skin. Always a peaceful meditation.

We are strolling through the delightful gardens of Eden. Birds serenely chirping and singing ... butterflies dancing among luminous flowers ... towering trees offering tranquillity and sanctuary ... abundant lush plants ... psychedelic hummingbirds whirring in the gorgeous warmth ... rain quenching the landscape only from 2am - 4am ... a true paragon.

Amrita has requested the tribal meeting be held at the Ecstatic Tantra temple. When we arrive, she seats the twenty-six attendees at two large outdoor tables surrounded by roses, tulips, lilies and snapdragons. Truly beautiful backdrop.

I open the meeting.

"Welcome everyone. A few updates from Eva, then we'll discuss any last-minute issues."

She deftly explains the agreement with the gods, the impending arrival of more Gifted, the amended clothing policy, then finishes with gentle reminders of Eden's norms and culture.

Quiet reflective nods.

Klamath Elder Láshaltko: "Are we ready for the next phase?"

Terraformer: "Will North America and Canada still have states?"

Tantrika Amrita: "No borders, no poverty, no violence."

Engineer: "I propose 100 Quadrants, numbered left to right, north to south. The cities within each quadrant will be numbered in the same way."

The Entertainment Executive bursts into laughter. "I suppose my home address will read as follows: Quadrant 90, City 12, Tree 17, Home 9."

Engineer: "Landmass 1 for North America and Canada. Thus L1 Q90 C12 T17 H9."

Tantrika Amrita: "I like it. We're trying to get away from nationalism and regionalism. One Tribe, remember?"

The attendees quickly endorse the proposal.

Q'ero Shaman Akllasumaq: "I see birds, butterflies, bees ... Where are the animals?"

Zoologist: "We will create vast open ranges allowing animals to roam freely in their natural habitat. These will be located between cities, securely shielded from human citizens. Innumerable nano-cameras will feed images constantly into the lume system. Observational expeditions will be permitted, provided they do not disrupt or stress the animals."

African Shaman Iboga smiles. "It's a new era."

Buddhist Monk Sangye: "Peace and kindness to all living beings."

Aboriginal Elder Mandu: "Long overdue. Awesome plan."

The second proposal is swiftly approved.

Sikh Nanak gestures enthusiastically. "The temples are spectacular. So much awaits new Tribe members."

Imam Abu Talib: "Freedom from ideology and religion."

African Shaman Iboga: "Universal spiritual principles, expansion of consciousness, heightened-awareness states, other-dimensional realities."

Buddhist Monk Sangye: "Healing and transcendence."

Hopi Mystic Qaletaqa: "Meeting the Source. Embracing the Light."

Tantrika Amrita is dancing jubilantly. "Whoo hoo! I love it!"

Zen Master Koichi raises his hand.

All eyes fall upon him.

"Amrita and I are getting married."

Ebullient applause and congratulations.

Sikh Nanak: "When is the event?"

Tantrika Amrita: "At sunset. You are all invited."

I wait until everyone settles.

"Any other issues?"

Christian Mystic Francis: "Will the 144,000 be spread throughout the planet?"

Eva: "Yes. As Eden expands, they will relocate."

Scientist: "How fast will Eden expand?"

Eva: "Very quickly into uninhabited areas. The gods will clear the way."

Landscaper: "Eden will eventually cover the entire planet?"

Eva: "Yes. One Tribe. One Planet."

I gaze across the tables.

Sparkling silence.

"Alright. That's a wrap. Let's get ready for a wedding."

The sun is low on the horizon. Golden streaks glimmer across the verdant landscape. We are gathered on the hill near the Tantra Temple.

African Shaman Iboga is leading the ceremony.

Zen Master Koichi and Tantrika Amrita are sitting in Yab-Yum, the paramount Tantric position in which the man sits cross-legged with the woman on his lap and her legs wrapped around him. Yab-Yum, from the Tibetan 'father-mother', represents the primordial union of wisdom and compassion.

After a brief inspiriting oration, Iboga raises a vibrant autumn-coloured ribbon to the heavens. She invokes a blessing from the ancestors and beings of light. The marrying couple's right hands are fastened. They are invited to declare their vows.

The ambience is heartfelt and joyful.

"Today I take you to be my husband. I promise to immerse you in the ways of Ecstatic Tantra. To share with you the *juiciness* of Tantra, the *nurturing* of Tantra and the *unconditional love* of Tantra. I vow to walk with you in Surrender, Trust and Flow. I pledge to grow old by your side as your best friend and kindred spirit. For all eternity."

"Today I take you to be my wife. I promise to immerse you in the ways of Ecstatic Existence. To share with you the *juiciness* of Existence, the *nurturing* of Existence and the *unconditional love* of Existence. I vow to walk with you in Surrender, Trust and Flow. I pledge to grow old by your side as your best friend and kindred spirit. For all eternity."

Amrita leans forward and kisses him passionately. They embrace tightly. Her ardent whisper is barely audible: "Pashatos."

Ah. Śakra taught her a few sacred words too. It belongs to the mysterious language that engenders exquisite and powerful thought-forces. Highly secretive and rarely shared.

Hmm. Intriguing.

Iboga closes the ceremony: "And so it is."

Everyone intones "And so it is."

Rush of exultant handshakes, hugs and kisses.

After a few minutes the Tribe follows the newlyweds to the Tantra Temple.

Eva and I linger on the hilltop, our recent nuptials fresh in our consciousness.

The glory of Eden shimmers before us.

She shakes her head.

"We've come so far."

Touch her shoulder gently.

"Vision, strategy, action."

"Love, surrender, trust."

My robe flickers a red signal.

"Gifted knocking at the door."

"Purrfect timing."

She summons Anunaki.

How may I serve?

"The expansion of Eden is about to commence. You have the blueprints, protocols and parameters. Are you ready to build more cities?"

Awaiting your command.

Eva waves her fingers.

"A new world begins. Make it so."

The sky is painting a rainbow of luminous colours.

Her hand slips lovingly into mine.

We stand enraptured.

A tranquil whisper.

"Do you think anyone has worked it out yet?"

I turn my head and smile.

"Jesus Christ?"

"Yeah."

"In time."

"Meanwhile ..."

"One Tribe."

"One Love."

"One Planet."

Stephen Shaw's Books

Visit the website: www.i-am-stephen-shaw.com

I Am contains spiritual and mystical teachings from enlightened masters that point the way to love, peace, bliss, freedom and spiritual awakening.

Heart Song takes you on a mystical adventure into creating your reality and manifesting your dreams, and reveals the secrets to attaining a fulfilled and joyful life.

They Walk Among Us is a love story spanning two realities. Explore the mystery of the angels. Discover the secrets of Love Whispering.

The Other Side explores the most fundamental question in each reality. What happens when the physical body dies? Where do you go? Expand your awareness. Journey deep into the Mystery.

Reflections offers mystical words for guidance, meditation and contemplation. Open the book anywhere and unwrap your daily inspiration.

5D is the Fifth Dimension. Discover ethereal doorways hidden in the fabric of space-time. Seek the advanced mystical teachings.

Star Child offers an exciting glimpse into the future on earth. The return of the gods and the advanced mystical teachings. And the ultimate battle of light versus darkness.

The Tribe expounds the joyful creation of new Earth. What happened after the legendary battle of Machu Picchu? What is Christ consciousness? What is Ecstatic Tantra?

The Fractal Key reveals the secrets of the shamans. This handbook for psychonauts discloses the techniques and practices used in psychedelic healing and transcendent journeys.